Joey Green's
Rainy Day Magic

Other Books by Joey Green

Hellbent on Insanity
The Gilligan's Island Handbook
The Get Smart Handbook
The Partridge Family Album
Polish Your Furniture with Panty Hose
Hi Bob!
Selling Out
Paint Your House with Powdered Milk
Wash Your Hair with Whipped Cream
The Bubble Wrap Book
Joey Green's Encyclopedia of Offbeat Uses for Brand-Name Products
The Zen of Oz
The Warning Label Book
Monica Speaks
The Official Slinky Book
You Know You've Reached Middle Age If . . .
The Mad Scientist Handbook
Clean Your Clothes with Cheez Whiz
The Road to Success Is Paved with Failure
Clean It! Fix It! Eat It!
Joey Green's Magic Brands
The Mad Scientist Handbook 2
Senior Moments
Jesus and Moses: The Parallel Sayings
Joey Green's Amazing Kitchen Cures
Jesus and Muhammad: The Parallel Sayings
Joey Green's Gardening Magic
How They Met
Joey Green's Incredible Country Store
Potato Radio, Dizzy Dice
Joey Green's Supermarket Spa
Weird Christmas
Contrary to Popular Belief
Marx & Lennon: The Parallel Sayings

Joey Green's
Rainy Day Magic

**443 Fun, Simple Projects to Do with Kids
Using Brand-Name Products
You've Already Got Around the House**

JOEY GREEN

Copyright © 2006 by Joey Green

First published in the USA in 2006 by

Fair Winds Press, a member of Quayside Publishing Group

33 Commercial Street

Gloucester, MA 01930

10 09 08 07 06   2 3 4 5

ISBN - 13: 978-1-59233-204-5

ISBN - 10: 1-59233-204-8

Library of Congress Cataloging-in-Publication Data

Green, Joey.

  Rainy day magic : 443 fun, simple projects to do with kids using brand-name products you've already got around the house / Joey Green.

    p. cm.

  Includes index.

  ISBN 1-59233-204-8

  1. Handicraft--Juvenile literature. 2. Brand name products--Juvenile literature. I. Title.

  TT160.G8145 2006

  745.5--dc22   2006000441

Cover photography by Ken Chernus

Cover design by Laura McFadden

Book design by Joey Green

Photography by Joey Green

Printed in Canada

For Julia

Ingredients

But First, a Word from Our Sponsor

Ever been trapped inside on a rainy day with a houseful of kids? Not only do they need constant attention, but after a while, they start to go stir-crazy, bouncing off the walls. You open up an arts and crafts book only to discover that you don't have half of the necessary ingredients, and you're not about to head out in a torrential downpour to buy plaster of Paris, poster paint, modeling clay, or glitter. So what can you possibly do?

The truth is: you don't have to run out to an arts supply store to do crafts projects with the kids. Using common brand-name products that you've already got around the house—in the kitchen, under the bathroom sink, in the laundry room, and around the garage—you can come up with a multitude of astonishing rainy day projects on the spur of the moment that kids truly love and that quickly turn you into the most amazing parent in the world. With an ordinary box of Forster Toothpicks and a bottle of Elmer's Glue-All, a kid can become a junior civil engineer, building an elaborate bridge. You can delight children by making finger paints with Gillette Foamy Shaving Cream and McCormick Food Coloring. Or make homemade play dough with Gold Medal Flour and Morton Salt. It's as easy as pie. Actually, it's much easier than baking a pie.

How did I come up with all these rainy day activities? Well, as a teenager I worked as an arts and crafts counselor, in college I majored in Fine Arts, and at present, I have two daughters and fourteen nieces and nephews—so I've spent plenty of time cooped up in the house on rainy days with nothing to entertain them but a box of Glad Drinking Straws and a roll of Scotch Tape. On top of all that, I've become the guru of offbeat uses for brand-name products, so the kids expect me to conjure up dozens of fun activities using nothing more than the boxes of Jell-O, Carnation Nonfat Dry Milk, and Kraft Macaroni & Cheese lying around the house. When did I decide to write this book? Perhaps it was on that rainy afternoon when the kids were jumping up and down on the sofas, preparing to launch a water balloon fight in my living room.

So I experimented with scores of brand-name products we all know and love. I cooked up homemade play dough over the kitchen stove, crafted papier-mâché with Gold Medal Flour, painted watercolor pictures with Kool-Aid, created sand art with Jell-O, and made necklaces with Kellogg's Froot Loops and Oral-B Dental Floss. But the rain wouldn't stop. So I learned how to make glue from Uncle Ben's Converted Brand Rice, discovered how to build a gingerbread house using Honey Maid Graham Crackers and Marshmallow Fluff, and tie-dyed my kids' T-shirts with Tang. When the rain finally let up, I contacted manufacturers to obtain their secret files, talked with dozens of artists and craftspeople, and searched through the hundreds of e-mails I receive through my Web site, www.wackyuses.com where innovative Moms and Dads like you share their insanely brilliant uses for brand-name products with me.

I was thunderstruck by some incredibly unique and simple rainy day projects. You can make a model aquarium with Pepperidge Farm Goldfish. Tide doubles as black-light paint. You can marble paper with Gillette Foamy Shaving Cream and McCormick Food Coloring. You can build a homemade rocket with Alka-Seltzer. You can make lip gloss with Crisco All-Vegetable Shortening. You can put together beanbags with L'eggs Sheer Energy Panty Hose, create jewelry from Wonder Bread, and carve a block of SPAM into the Venus de Milo. Along the way, I also learned some surprising facts, like who invented Kool-Aid, how Barbie got her name, and what's so crazy about Krazy Glue.

This book is the result of too many rainy days stuck inside the house with a group of restless kids and my desperate attempts to prevent them from sticking unwrapped slices of Kraft American Cheese into my brand-new DVD player. Inside you'll discover a smorgasbord of practical yet quirky ways to foster creativity, keep your kids entertained, and be a great parent. Excuse me now, while I go shampoo the cherry Kool-Aid out of my hair.

Banks and Coins

Coin Bank
● **Gerber Baby Food.** To make a coin bank, remove the lid from a clean, empty jar of Gerber Baby Food and (with adult supervision) use a screwdriver and a hammer to punch a coin slot in the center of the lid. To decorate the jar, paint or glue glitter, colored rice (see page 109), or colored macaroni (see page 109) to the outside of the glass jar. Let dry, and then screw on the lid.

Coin Cleaner
● **Coca-Cola.** To clean tarnished pennies, fill a drinking glass with Coca-Cola and drop in the pennies. Let sit for one hour, and then wipe clean with a soft cloth.

● **Heinz Ketchup.** Pour a thick coat of Heinz Ketchup over tarnished pennies, let sit for an hour, and then wash off. The acids from the tomatoes and vinegar in the ketchup clean the tarnish so the copper shines like new.

● **Heinz White Vinegar** and **Arm & Hammer Baking Soda.** Fill a clean jar with Heinz White Vinegar, and then add one teaspoon Arm & Hammer Baking Soda. Stir well, and then drop the coins into the jar and let soak overnight. In the morning, rinse the coins clean with water.

● **ReaLemon** and **Morton Salt.** Wet a clean cloth with ReaLemon lemon juice, and then dip the wet cloth into Morton Salt and rub a copper penny gently until it sparkles. (Or mix ReaLemon lemon juice with Morton Salt in a small Tupperware container. Add the dirty pennies. Seal the lid, shake well for two minutes, and then let sit for five minutes. Remove the pennies, rinse under warm water, and dry.

● **Tabasco Pepper Sauce.** Wet a clean, soft cloth with Tabasco Pepper Sauce and wipe the tarnished pennies until they come clean.

Money Snake

● **L'eggs Sheer Energy Panty Hose.** With adult supervision, use a pair of scissors to cut off one leg from a clean, used pair of L'eggs Sheer Energy Panty Hose. Fill the leg with coins and secure the open end with a rubber band or hair band, so you can always add more coins until you've filled the panty hose leg, creating a long, money snake.

Papier-Mâché Bank

● **Gold Medal Flour, *USA Today,*** and **Dixie Cups.** Inflate a balloon to the size you want your bank to be and tie a knot in the neck of the balloon. Mix one cup Gold Medal Flour with two-thirds cup water in a medium-size bowl to a thick-glue consistency. To thicken, add more flour. With adult supervision, use a pair of scissors to cut *USA Today* into strips approximately one to two inches in width. Dip each strip into the paste, gently pull it between your fingers to remove excess paste, and apply it to the balloon, leaving the knot exposed. Repeat until you have covered the balloon with three to four layers of newspaper strips. If you want to create a piggy bank, attach a Dixie Cup to one end of the balloon to create a snout and cover with several layers of newspaper strips. You can also make legs, ears, a tail, and facial features, if you wish. Set the balloon on the mouth of a second paper cup and let dry completely. Pop the balloon and cover the hole with masking tape or more papier-mâché. Cut a slot in the top of the bank. Decorate with poster paint. You can also glue on buttons for eyes or decorate with colored rice (see page 109) or glitter. After the paint dries, coat with shellac.

Piggy Bank

● **Clorox Bleach jug, Krazy Glue,** and **Kodak Film canisters.** To make a piggy bank, with adult supervision, use a knife to cut a slot in the middle of the side of a clean, empty Clorox Bleach jug in line with the handle and use Krazy Glue to glue four empty Kodak 35 mm Film canisters upside down to the opposite side to create legs. Then decorate the bottle by gluing on shapes cut from colored construction paper or felt. Or simply use the upright jug as a bank and decorate.

● **Coca-Cola bottle, Krazy Glue, Kodak Film canisters,** and **Elmer's Glue-All.** With adult supervision, use a knife to cut a coin slot in the middle of the side of a clean, empty two-liter plastic Coca-Cola bottle. Using Krazy Glue, adhere four Kodak 35 mm Film canisters upside down to the opposite side of the bottle to create four legs. Using Elmer's Glue-All, glue to the bottle shapes cut from colored construction paper to create ears, eyes, spots, and a curlicue tail for the piggy bank. Glue a small circle of construction paper to the top of the bottle cap to create a nose for the pig.

STRANGE FACTS

● During the Middle Ages, Western Europeans used pygg, an orange clay, to fashion jars, pots, and plates. People saved their money in pygg jars, which became known in eighteenth century England as pig jars or pig banks, prompting potters to fashion the jars into the shape of pigs.

● In the New Testament, Jesus warns against giving pearls to swine (Matthew 7:6), yet tossing coins into a piggy bank is literally doing just that.

● In 1864, United States Secretary of the Treasury Salmon P. Chase put the phrase "In God We Trust" on some United States coins to boost morale during the Civil War. In 1955, Congress ordered that the phrase appear on all United States coins and paper money. In 1956, Congress made the phrase the official United States. national motto.

● Before he became a bank robber, John Dillinger was a local baseball star in Martinsville, Indiana, playing shortstop. He teamed up with the umpire as his first partner in crime.

Bathtub Fun

Back Scrubber
● **L'eggs Sheer Energy Panty Hose** and **Ivory Soap.** Cut off the leg of a pair of used L'eggs Sheer Energy Panty Hose, stick a bar of Ivory Soap inside at the knee, tie a knot around both ends, and seesaw the panty hose across your back.

Bath Fizzies
● **Arm & Hammer Baking Soda, Country Time Lemonade, Kingsford's Corn Starch, Johnson's Baby Oil, McCormick Food Coloring,** and **Reynolds Cut-Rite Wax Paper.** Mix four teaspoons Arm & Hammer Baking Soda, two teaspoons unsweetened Country Time Lemonade drink mix, and one teaspoon Kingford's Corn Starch in a bowl. Mix four teaspoons Johnson's Baby Oil and three to six drops McCormick Food Coloring in a second bowl. Slowly mix the colored oil into the bowl of mixed powders, blending well. Make small balls (roughly one inch in diameter) of the mixture. Place on a sheet of Reynolds Cut-Rite Wax Paper and let dry completely for 24 to 48 hours. To use, fill your bathtub with water and drop in a couple of bath fizzies.

Bath Toys
● **SueBee Honey.** Use a clean, empty SueBee Honey bear as a bath toy in the bathtub.

Blue Bath
● **Mrs. Stewart's Liquid Bluing.** Add a few drops of Mrs. Stewart's Liquid Bluing in the bath water to turn the water blue, enticing kids to get into the tub. Mrs. Stewart's Liquid Bluing, a fine blue iron powder suspended in water, is nontoxic and biodegradable.

Boat that Floats

● **Ivory Soap** and **Forster Toothpicks.**
With adult supervision, use a regular flatware knife (or a plastic knife) to carve a bar of Ivory Soap into the shape of a boat, hollowing out the center to create the seating area. Insert a Forster Toothpick into the center of the soap to create a mast for the sail, which you can fashion from a small square cut from a piece of colored construction paper.

Bubble Bath

● **Clairol Herbal Essences Shampoo.** To make bubble bath, pour one capful Clairol Herbal Essences Shampoo under a running tap in the bathtub for an all-natural bubble bath with massive amounts of bubbles.

● **Dawn Dishwashing Liquid.** Add a few drops of Dawn Dishwashing Liquid to running bath water to create a tub full of bubbles.

● **Ivory Soap.** Hold a bar of Ivory Soap under a running faucet to fill the tub with bubbles.

● **Johnson's Baby Oil** and **Johnson's Baby Shampoo.**
Combine two cups Johnson's Baby Oil and two tablespoons Johnson's Baby Shampoo. Mix the solution in a blender at high speed. Add to running bath water.

Car Washing

● **Ivory Dishwashing Liquid.** If you can't get your kids to take a bath, have them wash the car instead, which ends up getting them covered with soap bubbles from head to toe. Add two teaspoons Ivory Dishwashing Liquid to a bucket of water to wash your car and let them go crazy.

Shaving Cream Madness

● **Gillette Foamy Shaving Cream.** For lots of bathtub fun, use a can of Gillette Foamy Shaving Cream to draw on the bathtub walls. The shaving cream washes right off with water and doubles as soap.

Soap Crayons

● **Ivory Snow** and **McCormick Food Coloring.** Mix 1-3/4 cup Ivory Snow (powder) and one-quarter cup water in a large bowl to the consistency of pudding. Add fifty drops McCormick Food Coloring and blend well. Scoop the mixture into a plastic ice-cube tray, pressing the paste into the compartments. Set the ice-cube tray in a warm, dry spot and let dry for up to 48 hours or until the soap cubes harden. Pop the soap cubes out of the ice-cube tray and use the soap crayons to write on the bathtub, the tile wall in the bathtub stall, and on your body. The colored soap washes right off.

STRANGE FACTS

● By 3000 B.C.E., Pakistanis had private bathtubs in their homes with taps and terra-cotta pipes.

● While taking a bath, Greek scientist Archimedes realized that his body, immersed in water, lost weight equal to the weight of the water it displaced. This law of physics is known as the Archimedean principle.

● Since full-body bathing required nudity, the Catholic Church labeled the activity as sinful, banning this temptation of the flesh and putting an end to regular bathing throughout Europe. Without good hygiene, diseases like the Black Plague spread like wildfire, killing thousands.

● French playwright Edmond Rostand wrote his 1898 play *Cyrano de Bergerac* while sitting in a bathtub.

● William Howard Taft, weighing three hundred pounds, was the only United States President to get stuck in the White House bathtub.

● In 1964, astronaut John Glenn fell in the bathtub, forcing him to withdraw from his race for senator from Ohio. Glenn was elected to the Senate in 1974.

Batik

● **Crayola Crayons.** Using a white Crayola Crayon, draw a design on a piece of white paper. Use watercolors or tempera paint to paint over the paper. The wax crayon resists the paint, allowing you to create an unusual design. You can also experiment using different colored crayons. To create an even more unusual design, crinkle up the piece of paper and flatten it out before painting it.

● **Crayola Crayons, Playtex Living Gloves, Kool-Aid, Heinz White Vinegar,** *USA Today,* and **Bounty Paper Towels.** With adult supervision, melt several white (or light colored) Crayola Crayons by putting them in a tin can and putting the can in a saucepan full of water, and then heating the water on the stove. When the wax melts to liquid, put on a pair of Playtex Living Gloves and carefully use a paintbrush dipped in the melted wax to paint designs on a plain, white, 100-percent cotton T-shirt or piece of cloth. Make sure you paint the wax on thickly so it will block the dye, leaving you with clean white lines. Let dry.

For each color you wish to use, mix the contents of one package Kool-Aid and one ounce Heinz White Vinegar in individual plastic bowls until dissolved. Wearing Playtex Living Gloves, dip the cloth into the Kool-Aid dye or use a paintbrush to paint the Kool-Aid solution onto the cloth. Let dry. When completely dry, cover a section of *USA Today* newspaper with Bounty Paper Towels, place the cloth wax-side down on top of the paper towels, and (with adult supervision) iron the cloth. The heat from the iron will melt the wax, and the paper towels will absorb the wax. To set colors, let the cloth set for twenty-four hours before laundering. To avoid running colors, wash separately the first time. Launder as usual, and it's ready to wear.

● **Elmer's Glue-All.** Gently squeezing the glue from a bottle of Elmer's Glue-All, draw a design on a piece of white paper. Let dry. Use watercolors to paint over the glue on the paper. The glue resists the watercolors, creating a beautiful design.

● **Gold Medal Flour, McCormick Alum, Ziploc Storage Bags,** and **Bounty Paper Towels.** You can batik T-shirts or pillowcases (using fabric paints so the colors won't wash out) or make a wall hanging. With adult supervision, mix one-half cup Gold Medal Flour, one-half cup water, and two teaspoons McCormick Alum in a blender. Fill a Ziploc Storage Bag with the flour solution, seal the bag shut, and snip off a bottom corner of the bag with a pair of scissors. Squeezing the flour solution from the hole in the bag, draw a design on a piece of prewashed white cloth. (If you prefer, you can use a clean, empty Dawn Dishwashing Liquid bottle instead of a Ziploc Storage Bag.) If you wish, you can draw a design on a piece of paper, place the design under the cloth, and trace over it. Let the cloth dry overnight. When the flour paste is dry on the cloth, spread several layers of Bounty Paper Towels on a table, place the cloth on top of it, and use watercolors to paint the open areas on the cloth. Remember, the colors will dry lighter than they appear, so use thick coats of paint. Let dry overnight. When the cloth is completely dry, rub the cloth with your fingers to crack off all the dried flour paste. The flour paste will have blocked the paint from coloring the fabric in the areas previously covered with the paste. If the cloth is wrinkled, have an adult iron it.

Other Fabric Dyes

● **Lipton Tea** and **Playtex Living Gloves.** Brew a pot of really strong tea, using several Lipton Tea Bags. Wearing Playtex Living Gloves, dip the cloth into the hot tea. Let dry.

● **Maxwell House Coffee** and **Playtex Living Gloves.** Brew two pots of Maxwell House Coffee and pour into a large Rubbermaid box. Wearing Playtex Living Gloves, dip the cloth into the hot coffee. Let dry.

● **Tang, Heinz White Vinegar, and Playtex Living Gloves.** Mix one-half cup Tang powdered drink mix and one ounce Heinz White Vinegar in a bowl until dissolved. Wearing Playtex Living Gloves, dip the cloth into the orange solution. To set colors, with adult supervision iron the cloth of garment on medium-high, placing an ironing cloth between the cloth and the iron. Let set for 24 hours before washing. To avoid running colors, wash separately the first time.

● **Welch's 100% Purple Grape Juice** and **Playtex Living Gloves.** Pour one cup Welch's Grape Juice into a bowl. Wearing Playtex Living Gloves, dip the cloth into the grape juice. To set colors, with adult supervision iron the cloth of garment on medium-high, placing an ironing cloth between the cloth and the iron. Let set for 24 hours before washing. To avoid running colors, wash separately the first time.

STRANGE FACTS

● Archeologists have found evidence of batiks in the Far East, Middle East, Central Asia, and India dating back to more than two thousand years ago.

● Scholars speculate that the art of batik originated in Asia and spread south to the islands of the Malay Archipelago and west to the Middle East through the caravan route.

● The Chinese practiced the art of batik on silk cloth as early as the Sui Dynasty (581–618 c.e.).

● For centuries, the Yoruba tribe of Southern Nigeria and Senegal has practiced the art of batik using cassava and rice paste.

● The art of batik has reached the highest level of expertise on the Indonesian island of Java, most notably in the city of Yogyakarta.

● In 1835, the Dutch brought Indonesian craftsmen to the Netherlands to teach the craft of batik to artisans in several factories in Holland.

Birds

Bird Feeders

● **Clorox Bleach jug, Hartz Parakeet Seed,** and **Oral-B Dental Floss.** Wash an empty Clorox Bleach jug thoroughly with water and a few drops of dishwashing liquid and air dry for several days. With adult supervision, cut a hole in the side of the jug opposite the handle. Fill the bottom of the jug with Hartz Parakeet Seed and hang the bird feeder from a tree branch with a loop of Oral-B Dental Floss.

● **Elmer's Glue-All, Reynolds Cut-Rite Wax Paper, Hartz Parakeet Seed,** and **Oral-B Dental Floss.** Remove the cap from a bottle of Elmer's Glue-All and squeeze out a thick, squiggly line (overlapping itself if you wish) onto a sheet of Reynolds Cut-Rite Wax Paper. Using a spoon, sprinkle Hartz Parakeet Seed over the squiggly glue line, covering all the glue. Let dry overnight. Tilt the wax paper to let the excess bird seed spill off, and then carefully peel off the wax paper. Tie a piece of Oral-B Dental Floss to the hardened glue squiggle to hang it outdoors.

● **Jif Peanut Butter, Hartz Parakeet Seed,** and **Oral-B Dental Floss.** Spoon Jif Peanut Butter between the petals of a large pine cone, and then roll the peanut butter-coated pine cone in Hartz

Parakeet Seed. Hang the birdseed-coated pine cone outdoors with a piece of Oral-B Dental Floss.

● **SueBee Honey, Hartz Parakeet Seed,** and **Oral-B Dental Floss.** Punch a hole in the top of an empty cardboard tube (from a used roll of toilet paper or paper towels). Roll the cardboard tube in SueBee Honey, and then roll the honey-coated tube in Hartz Parakeet Seed. Hang the birdseed-coated tube outdoors with a piece of Oral-B Dental Floss. (Instead of a cardboard tube, you can also use a large pinecone.)

Birdbath

● **Frisbee.** With adult supervision, punch three equidistant holes along the circumference of the Frisbee, insert wire, and hang the Frisbee upside down from a tree or post. Fill with water or let the rain do it naturally.

STRANGE FACTS

● To stay airborne, birds must fly at an average speed of eleven miles per hour.

● The song of the white-breasted wren of Mexico sounds like Beethoven's Fifth Symphony.

● Fear of birds is called ornithophobia.

● Crows can be domesticated as pets and sometimes taught to speak a few words, like parrots.

● Hummingbirds, able to fly backwards, sideways, and upside down, cannot walk.

● Eggs do not crush under the weight of a mother bird as she sits on the nest because when a force is applied to an egg, the curve of the egg distributes the force over a wide area away from the point of contact.

● In Alfred Hitchcock's 1963 movie *The Birds*—starring Rod Taylor, Tippi Hedren, Jessica Tandy, and Suzanne Pleshette—thousands of birds violently attack people in a quaint New England town. When asked by a reporter how he got the birds to act so well, Hitchcock replied, "They were very well paid, ma'am."

Bubbles

Black-Light Bubbles

● **Liquid Tide.** You can make bubbles with Liquid Tide that glow under black light. Simply dilute the Liquid Tide with enough water to make bubbles. Liquid Tide contains a fluorescent chemical that is activated by the ultraviolet rays produced by a black light. The fluorescent chemical in the Liquid Tide converts the ultraviolet light into visible light.

Bubble Formulas

● **Dawn** (or **Joy**) **Dishwashing Liquid** and **Karo Light Corn Syrup.** Mix one-quarter cup Dawn (or Joy) Dishwashing Liquid, one tablespoon Karo Light Corn Syrup, and 30 ounces distilled or soft water (not hard water) in a shallow bowl or a pie tin.

● **Dawn** (or **Joy**) **Dishwashing Liquid** and **Karo Light Corn Syrup.** For enormous monster bubbles, mix two cups Dawn (or Joy) Dishwashing Liquid, one cup Karo Light Corn Syrup, and four cups distilled or soft water (not hard water) to use with big bubble wands.

Bubble Machine

● **Cool Whip tub, Glad Flexible Straws,** and **Dawn Dishwashing Liquid.** Using a hole puncher, punch a hole in the top edge of a clean, empty Cool Whip canister. Punch a second hole in the edge of the plastic lid. Insert a Glad Flexible Straw in the side hole, flexible end first, so the straw is bent toward the floor of the tub. Pour one teaspoon Dawn Dishwashing Liquid into the Cool Whip container, and then fill halfway with water. Stir well with a spoon. Carefully snap the lid closed, positioning the hole in the lid directly opposite the hole in the side of the container. Blow through the straw. A surplus of bubbles will surge through the hole in the lid.

Bubble Tools

- **Bounty Paper Towels.** You can blow bubbles using the cardboard tube from a roll of Bounty Paper Towels. Simply dip one end of the cardboard tube in the bubble solution, raise into the air, and blow through the other end of the tube.

- **Budweiser Beer.** Dip the plastic holder from a six pack of Budweiser Beer cans into the solution and use it to blow bubbles.

- **Charmin Toilet Paper.** You can blow bubbles using the cardboard tube from a roll of Charmin Toilet Paper. Simply dip one end of the cardboard tube in the bubble solution, raise into the air, and blow through the other end of the tube.

- **Glad Drinking Straws.** With adult supervision, diagonally cut the end of a Glad Drinking Straw, dip into bubble soap, and blow.

- **Glad Drinking Straws.** With adult supervision, use a needle to thread a three-foot length of string through two plastic Glad Drinking Straws as if beading a necklace. Knot the ends of the string together and glide the knot inside one of the two straws. Hold the two plastic drinking straws apart so the string is taut, dip it in the bubble solution, and then lift up while simultaneously bringing the straws together.

STRANGE FACTS

● A soap bubble is a drop of water that has been stretched out into a sphere by using soap to loosen the magnetic attraction that exists between water molecules. Glycerin helps gives the walls of the bubble strength. When blowing bubbles, the air pushes apart the molecules in the soapy film, but the molecules, attracted to each other, contract, forming the smallest surface possible to contain the largest volume of air possible—a sphere.

● The surface tension of a soap bubble is uniform for the entire bubble.

● Bubbles filled with carbon dioxide (blown from your mouth) last longer than bubbles filled with air.

● Bubbles made from a warm soapy solution last nearly twice as a long as bubbles made from a cold soapy solution. Warmth sustains the surface tension of the bubbles. With adult supervision, warm the bubble solution by placing it in a pot and heating it to 120 degrees Fahrenheit.

● The more detergent used to make the bubble solution, the larger the bubbles will be. Using a bubble formula that calls for more detergent than water enables you to create monstrous bubbles.

● Adding glycerin, corn syrup, or sugar to a bubble formula slows down the evaporation of the water in the bubble, making the bubbles last longer.

● Bubbles blown on a rainy day last longer due to the moisture in the air.

● By wetting one end of a plastic straw in bubble mix, you can gently push it through a large bubble and then blow a second bubble inside the first bubble.

● The study of bubbles is called bubbleology.

Candles

Candles

● **Crisco All-Vegetable Shortening** (or **Pam Cooking Spray**), **Dannon Yogurt, Maxwell House Coffee, Crayola Crayons,** and **Forster Toothpicks.** Make a candle wick (see "Wicks" on page 21) or buy candle wick at a crafts store. Cover your work area with newspaper. Rub a thin coat of Crisco All-Vegetable Shortening (or spray a small amount of Pam Cooking Spray) on the inside of a clean, empty Dannon Yogurt cup. Place the plastic cup on a cookie tin or aluminum pan just in case the mold leaks or topples over accidentally. Prepare a cooling bath by filling a plastic or metal pan with enough water to come up to the level of the wax you intend to pour into the

yogurt cup. Wrap one end of your wick around the center of a pencil and lay the pencil across the top of the mold so the free end of the wick hangs to the bottom center of the plastic yogurt cup. Make sure the wick is taut.

With adult supervision, use a hammer and chisel to break a block of paraffin wax into small chunks. Put enough wax into a clean, empty Maxwell House Coffee can to fill the yogurt cup mold. With adult supervision in a well ventilated kitchen, fill the bottom of a pot halfway with water and bring to a boil. Place a trivet (or upside-down coffee cup) in the bottom of the pot to prevent the coffee can from sitting on the bottom of the pot.

When the water comes to a boil, set the coffee can on the trivet (or upside-down coffee cup) in the pot. Using this double-boiler method, the wax will not exceed a temperature above the boiling point of water—as long as you do not boil away all the water.

When the wax melts in the coffee can, drop a small piece of Crayola Crayon (any color you wish) into the liquid wax. Using a spoon, stir until the crayon dissolves. (To get an accurate idea of what color the wax will appear when it dries, carefully place a few small drops of the hot wax on a piece of white paper; if you're not satisfied with the color, melt more crayon into the liquid wax.)

When the colored wax is fully melted and colored, remove the wax from the heat, tilt the mold on a slight angle to avoid creating air bubbles and, wearing an oven mitt, slowly and smoothly pour the wax to within one-half inch of the top of the mold. (Always wear an oven mitt when handling molds filled with hot wax because the molds get very hot.) Save a cupful of wax for later.

Gently tap the sides of the mold with a spoon and wait one minute for any trapped air bubbles to rise to the surface.

Place the mold in the water bath, making sure no water runs into the mold. If necessary, set a weight (such as a saucer, a coffee mug, or a small book) across the top of the mold.

When a thin film forms across the top of the wax, remove the mold from the water bath and set on a level table. Since wax hardens from the outside toward the center, shrinking as it cools, a well will form around the wick. After forty-five minutes, insert a Forster Toothpick in three different places one inch from the wick to admit air into the void formed by the hardening wax. Reheat the cup of wax you set aside earlier until it melts into liquid and refill the well, being careful not to pour above the original wax level. (Overfilling the mold at this point will make removing the candle difficult and ruin the finish.)

Let the candle set in the mold overnight to cure fully. When both the mold and the wax are cool to the touch at room temperature, remove the pencil, hold the mold upside-down, and let the candle slide out.

If the candle does not slide out of the mold, place the mold in a refrigerator for twenty minutes, and then try again. As a last resort, hold the mold under hot running water until the candle slides out (softening the wax and usually marring the finish).

Trim the bottom of the candle with a knife. If the base of the candle is uneven, place a pie tin atop a pot of boiling water. Holding the candle by the wick, let it touch the heated pie tin until the base is flat and level. Cut the exposed wick to a length of one-half inch.

Dyes

● **Crayola Crayons.** When making candles with paraffin wax, melt a broken piece from a Crayola Crayon with the paraffin to make colored candles.

Lubricants

● **Crisco All-Vegetable Shortening.** Rub a thin coat of Crisco All-Vegetable Shortening on the inside of the candle mold before pouring in the hot wax so when the wax hardens, the candle will easily slide from the mold.

● **Pam Cooking Spray.** Spray a thin coat of Pam Cooking Spray on the inside of the candle mold before pouring in the hot wax. When the wax hardens, the oils from the cooking spray will enable the candle to easily slide from the mold.

Molds

● **Dannon Yogurt.** See "Candles" on pages 15–17.

● **Dixie Cups.** Tie one end of a four-inch string of wick to the middle of a pencil, set the pencil across the lip of a Dixie cup so the wick hangs to the bottom of the paper cup, pour melted paraffin wax to fill the cup, let harden, and you have an instant candle.

Candle Art

Aluminum Foil Candles

● **Glad Trash Bags** and **Reynolds Wrap.** Place a large, open rectangular plastic container, wooden box, or cardboard box inside a Glad Trash Bag, flatten the plastic to line the inside of the box, and fill the plastic-lined box with sand (collected from the beach or purchased from a hardware or garden supply store). Make an impression in the box of sand, place a sheet of Reynolds Wrap into it, and mold the foil to the shape, creating your candle mold. With adult supervision, add a wick and melt and pour the wax according to the directions on pages 15–17. When the candle hardens, peel off the foil.

Chunk Candles

● **Crisco All-Vegetable Shortening** (or **Pam Cooking Spray**).Oil a cookie sheet with Crisco All-Vegetable Shortening or Pam Cooking Spray and with adult supervision, melt the wax according to the directions on pages 15–17 and pour the melted wax into the cookie sheet to create chunks of whatever thickness you desire. Let cool until fairly hard, and then (with adult supervision) use a knife to slice the wax into squares (without removing them from the pan). Let cool completely, cut through the original slice marks, turn over the pan, and pop out the chunks. Repeat to make chunks of several different colors.

Prepare a mold and fill it with different chunks. Add a wick, melt some clear wax (without adding any color) and pour the wax into the mold, covering the chunks.

Ice Candles

● Fill a prepared mold with ice cubes or crushed ice, add a wick, and then pour melted wax over the ice, filling the mold. When the candle is removed, the melted ice will leave decorative pockets of air in the candle.

Layer Candles

● Prepare the mold with a wick and melt the wax according to the directions on pages 15–17. When the wax melts to liquid, pour a one-inch layer of colored wax into the mold. Place the mold in a water bath for a few minutes; remove it the moment the wax forms a firm, warm film across the surface. Heat a second can of wax, stir in a different color, and pour a second one-inch layer of wax into the mold. Place the mold in the cool water for a few minutes, remove, and continue this process until you fill the mold to the desired level.

Pour a combination of thick and thin layers or pour a multicolored stack of very thin layers. To make sure the layers adhere to each other, pour each additional layer before the previous layer has cooled.

To make tilted layer candles, tilt the mold on a block of wood and pour the first layer of wax. Before pouring the second layer, tilt the mold in a different direction. Continue this process until you are ready to pour the last layer, which should be done level to make the candle flat.

Mottled Candles

● **Johnson's Baby Oil.** Create small crystals in the wax by preparing the mold without lubrication, bringing the melted wax to 160 degrees Fahrenheit, and mixing in three tablespoons Johnson's Baby Oil for every pound of wax. (For more mottling, add more oil; for less mottling add less oil.) Immediately after stirring the oil into the wax, pour the wax into the mold to the desired level and cover with a paper bag or cardboard box so the wax cools slowly. (For more mottling, skip this step so the candle cools faster.) Do not place the mold in a water bath.

Sand Candles

● **Glad Trash Bags.** Place a large, open rectangular plastic container, wooden box, or cardboard box inside a Glad Trash Bag, flatten the plastic trash bag to line the inside of the box, and fill the plastic-lined box with sand (collected from the beach or purchased from a hardware or garden supply store). Mix enough water into the sand so that a small handful of the sand squeezed together retains its shape in your open palm without falling apart. Too much water will make the muddy sand stick to your hand.

Press a can, a block of wood, a bowl, a small ball, or a glass jar into the sand and pack the sand around it. Remove the object slowly, leaving an impression in the sand to be used as your candle mold.

To make legs on the candle, wrap a piece of tape around a wooden dowel one-half inch from an end and insert that end of the dowel into the sand in three spots (up to the end of the tape) to make holes of equal depth.

Wearing an oven mitt, hold a spoon in the middle of the hole-in-the-sand mold, and have an adult slowly pour the hot wax over the spoon so the wax does not erode the sand mold or splatter onto your hand. The wax will bubble and hiss as it contacts the wet sand. Fill the hole to the top with wax. Wax will seep into the sand, lowering the level of the wax roughly one inch.

Let the wax cool until a thick film forms on the surface. Use a knitting needle to poke a wick hole into the middle of the candle (without punching through the bottom), and insert a wire core wick into the hole, letting it extend above the surface of the sand.

When the wax hardens, remove the candle from the sand and lightly brush away the excess sand.

Hot Warnings

- Never leave melting wax unattended on a stove.
- Never heat wax beyond its flash point (usually about 375 degrees Fahrenheit for paraffin), otherwise the hot wax will combust, causing a fire.
- Keep wax away from open flames.
- Keep a pot lid, a box of Arm & Hammer Baking Soda, and a dry chemical fire extinguisher within easy reach when heating wax. Should the wax catch fire due to overheating, turn off the heat and smother the fire with the pot lid, baking soda, or fire extinguisher.
- Never put water on a wax fire. It causes the wax fire to spread.
- Fumes from overheated wax can cause severe illness, so in the event of an accident, ventilate and evacuate the area.
- Always use metal pot holders or pliers when handling hot pots or cans.
- Turn pot handles so they are not sticking out from the stovetop.
- If hot wax splashes on your skin, apply cold water immediately, and then peel off the wax.
- Never pour wax down a drain. It will clog the pipes.

Polishes

- **Bounty Paper Towels.** To remove blemishes from a candle, polish with a damp sheet of Bounty Paper Towel.
- **L'eggs Sheer Energy Panty Hose.** Polish a finished candle with a piece of nylon cut from a clean, used pair of L'eggs Sheer Energy Panty Hose. The nylon is a mild abrasive that gently smoothes blemishes from a candle.

Wicks

- **20 Mule Team Borax** and **Morton Salt.** To make your own wick, mix three tablespoons 20 Mule Team Borax, one tablespoon Morton Salt, and two cups water. Soak a cotton string in the solution for twenty-four hours. Let dry thoroughly, and then coat the string with paraffin wax (by dipping the string in melted wax) to eliminate air trapped between the fibers.

STRANGE FACTS

● The lit wick of a candle melts the surrounding wax. The porous wick absorbs the molten wax, which travels up the wick, feeding the flame with fuel.

● If a lit candle creates a minimal pool of wax and smokes excessively, the wick (absorbing too little molten wax) is too thick. If the wax pool formed by a lit candle drowns the wick or flows over the sides of the candle, the wick (absorbing too much molten wax) is too thin.

● A dripless candle is an ordinary candle made with a wick properly sized to consume all the wax.

● To make a thick wick, twist two thin wicks together (or braid three thin wicks together) and coat with hot wax.

● Candles colored with dyes sometime fade over time if exposed to direct sunlight or fluorescent lighting.

● Rolling candles in a sheet of Reynolds Cut-Rite Wax Paper before placing them in a drawer or storage box protects them from getting scuffed.

● Prevent wax from sticking to candle holders by giving the insides of candle holders a thin coat of Vaseline Petroleum Jelly.

● Remove candle wax from a table or countertop by blowing warm air with a blow dryer an inch above the drips, and then wiping away the wax with a Bounty Paper Towel.

● Elton John and Bernie Taupin reworded their song "Candle in the Wind," originally written about Marilyn Monroe, in tribute to Princess Diana. Elton sang the rewritten song at Diana's funeral. The song became the best-selling single of all time.

Cleanup Time

● **Bounty Paper Towels.** To remove candle wax from carpet or upholstery, place a sheet of Bounty Paper Towels over the wax. With adult supervision, gently press the paper towel with a warm iron. The iron will melt the wax, and the paper towel will absorb it.

Costumes and Masks

Beards
● **Johnson & Johnson Cotton Balls** and **Elmer's Glue-All.**
To make fake hair or beards, dip Johnson & Johnson
Cotton Balls in glue and
stick them to a paper bag,
a piece of construction
paper, or a bathing cap. (To
color cotton balls, add a few
drops of McCormick Food
Coloring to a bowl of water,
dip the cotton balls into the
water and drain. Place the
colored cotton balls on a sheet
of Reynolds Cut-Rite Wax
Paper and let dry.)

Body Paints
● **Crisco All-Vegetable Shortening** and **McCormick Food
Coloring.** Mix Crisco All-Vegetable Shortening with McCormick
Food Coloring in a muffin tin to make body paint in various colors.

Bunny Tail
● **Johnson & Johnson Cotton Balls.** Glue a handful of Johnson
& Johnson Cotton Balls to a small circle of white paper and pin it onto
a pair of white tights.

Clown Makeup
● **Kingsford's Corn Starch, Crisco All-Vegetable
Shortening,** and **McCormick Food Coloring.** To make white

clown face makeup, mix two tablespoons Kingsford's Corn Starch with one tablespoon Crisco All-Vegetable Shortening. For colored makeup, add a few drops of McCormick Food Coloring.

Face Glitter

● **Alberto VO5 Conditioning Hairdressing.** Glitter your face for a holiday party by rubbing a little Alberto VO5 Conditioning Hairdressing onto your cheeks, and then dust lightly with glitter.

Face Paint

● **Kingsford's Corn Starch, Noxzema,** and **McCormick Food Coloring.** For each color, mix one teaspoon Kingsford's Corn Starch, one-half teaspoon Noxzema, one-half teaspoon water, and several drops McCormick Food Coloring. Blend well with a spoon. Mix each color in its own compartment of a muffin tin.

Hair Dye

● **Kool-Aid.** Mix a thick paste using Kool-Aid and water, apply as you would hair dye, let sit five minutes, and then rinse. The result? Instant funky hair coloring that's nontoxic and washes out after a couple of shampoos.

● **Jell-O.** To color hair with Jell-O, make a thick paste from Jell-O powder and cold water, apply to hair, wait five minutes, and then rinse. It works great on light hair and washes out after a few shampoos.

● **McCormick Food Coloring.** To make your hair blue or green, squeeze a few drops of McCormick Food Coloring into your hair and comb it through until your achieve the desired color. The food coloring will wash out after a few shampoos.

● **Tang.** Mix Tang and a little water into a thick paste, apply to hair, wait five minutes, and then rinse. The orange coloring washes out after a few shampoos.

Halloween Makeup

● **Elmer's Glue-All** and **McCormick Food Coloring.** To simulate scars or burned skin, mix Elmer's Glue-All and a few drops of McCormick Food Coloring, apply to skin, and then let dry.

Hawaiian Grass Skirt
● **Glad Trash Bags.** Cut off the bottom of a Glad Trash Bag and cut long strips one inch wide to within three inches of the pull cord. Wear the skirt around your waist and secure the pull cord like a belt, tying a knot to keep the skirt in place.

Lip Gloss
● **Crisco All-Vegetable Shortening, Kool-Aid,** and **Kodak Film.** To make lip gloss, mix three tablespoons Crisco All-Vegetable Shortening and one package Kool-Aid (whatever flavor you like most) in a coffee cup. With adult supervision, microwave for one minute (or until the shortening melts to liquid). Carefully pour the colored liquid into a clean empty Kodak 35 mm Film canister, cap tightly, and refrigerate overnight. In the morning, you'll have homemade lip gloss in your favorite flavor.

Paper Plate Mask
● **Dixie Paper Plates, Crayola Crayons,** and **Oral-B Dental Floss.** With adult supervision, use a pair of scissors to cut out holes for eyes from a Dixie Paper Plate, color a face on the back of the plate with Crayola Crayons, punch two holes in the sides of the mask, and run a piece of Oral-B Dental Floss through the holes to create a strap to hold the mask in place on your face.

Papier-Mâché Mask
● **Gold Medal Flour** and *USA Today.* Mix one cup Gold Medal Flour with two-thirds cup water in a medium-size bowl to a thick-glue consistency. To thicken, add more flour. With adult supervision, use a pair of scissors to cut *USA Today* into strips approximately one to two inches in width. Blow up a balloon and tie a knot. Dip each strip of newspaper into the paste, gently pull it between your fingers to remove excess paste, and apply it to one side of the balloon, forming a nose and other facial features as desired. Let dry thoroughly. Pop the balloon. Use a pair of scissors to cut out eyes. Paint and texture as desired. Punch two holes on both sides of the mask's forehead and add a piece of yarn as a strap to wear the mask or hang it on a wall.

Robot Costume

● **Reynolds Wrap** and **Scotch Tape.** With adult supervision, use a pair of scissors to cut out a large U-shape from the front of a large, empty cereal box to wear the box on your head as a helmet. Wrap the box with Reynolds Wrap. For a spacesuit, wrap your body in sheets of Reynolds Wrap held in place with Scotch Tape. (You can also use silver face paint on your face to complete the robot look, if desired.)

Spiked Hair

● **Close-Up Classic Red Gel Toothpaste.** Rub a dollop of Close-Up Classic Red Gel Toothpaste in your hands, run your hands through your hair, and then comb your hair to achieve a spiky look. The toothpaste holds your hair in place, works for other hard-to-hold hairstyles as well, and leaves your hair kissably fresh.

● **Elmer's Glue-All.** Put a dab of Elmer's Glue-All the size of a quarter in your hand, rub in your hands, and apply evenly to your hair. Comb your hair with a fine-toothed comb to remove the excess glue. Now style spiked hair and let dry. (Elmer's Glue-All is water soluble and washes out of hair with regular shampoo.)

Viking Helmet

● **Gold Medal Flour,** *USA Today,* and **Pam Cooking Spray.** Mix one cup Gold Medal Flour with two-thirds cup water in a medium-size bowl to a thick-glue consistency. To thicken, add more flour. Cut *USA Today* into strips approximately one to two inches in width. Take a bowl that fits snugly on your head and spray the outside of the bowl with Pam Cooking Spray. Dip each newspaper strip into the paste, gently pull it between your fingers to remove excess paste, and apply it to the entire outer surface of the bowl. Let dry. Remove the papier-mâché cap from the bowl, using a butter knife to pry it free, if necessary. Use papier-mâché to add two horns to opposite sides of the cap. Let dry. Paint and texture as desired. If necessary, punch two holes beneath the horns to add a piece of yarn as a chin strap.

Wigs

● **L'eggs Sheer Energy Panty Hose.** Pull the waist of a clean, used pair of L'eggs Sheer Energy Panty Hose over your head like a hat, letting the legs flow as if they were braids.

STRANGE FACTS

● In the first Batman comic book, when millionaire Bruce Wayne decides to become a crime-fighting vigilante and tries to think up a costume that will strike fear into the hearts of his adversaries, a bat flies in his window, inspiring him to become Batman. He later creates a costume for his sidekick Robin, modeled after one of his favorite heroes, Robin Hood.

● In 1966, when called before the House Un-American Activities Committee (HUAC), Jerry Rubin, a political activist who had organized one of the first teach-ins against the war in Vietnam, showed up wearing the uniform of a 1776 American revolutionary.

● While trying to break into acting in Los Angeles, Brad Pitt worked for El Pollo Loco, a fast-food chain of Mexican restaurants, dressed in a chicken costume to greet customers.

● In William Shakespeare's play *Romeo and Juliet*, Romeo first spots Juliet at the Capulet family's annual masquerade party, which he attends disguised in a costume.

● In an episode of *The Partridge Family*, Mr. Kincaid arranges for the Partridge Family to star in a commercial for Uncle Erwin's Country Chicken, wearing feathered chicken suits.

Crayons and Chalk

Chalk Factory

● **Reynolds Cut-Rite Wax Paper** and **Scotch Tape.** For each stick of chalk you wish to make, line the inside of an empty toilet paper tube with Reynolds Cut-Rite Wax Paper and seal one end with Scotch Tape. In a bowl, mix two parts plaster of Paris with one part warm water with a spoon and add approximately two teaspoons tempera paint to achieve the desired color. Pour the mixture into the prepared toilet paper tubes. Gently tap the tubes to release air bubbles from the plaster. Repeat for each color of chalk you wish to make. Let the plaster mixture dry for forty-eight hours. Peel off the cardboard tube and wax paper.

Crayon Jar

● **Reynolds Wrap** and **Crayola Crayons.** Place a sheet of Reynolds Wrap shiny side up on a flat surface outside in hot, direct sunlight. Break several different colored Crayola Crayons into small pieces and sprinkle the pieces on the sheet of aluminum foil. Wait a few minutes for the crayons to melt, and then roll a clean, empty jar over the melted wax to coat the glass with unusual designs. Set the jar in a cool place, away from direct sunlight or heat, allowing the wax to harden. To finish off the jar, tie a ribbon around the neck of the jar and make a bow.

Crayon Resist

● **Crayola Crayons.** Using a white Crayola Crayon, draw a design on a piece of white paper. Use watercolors or tempera paint to paint over the paper. The wax crayon resists the paint, allowing you to create an unusual design. You can also experiment using different colored crayons. For more ways to make batiks, see page 7.

Crystal Paintings

● **Crayola Crayons** and **Epsom Salt.** Draw with Crayola Crayons on construction paper. Then, with adult supervision, mix together equal parts Epsom Salt and boiling water. Using a wide paintbrush, paint the picture with the salt mixture. When the picture dries, frosty crystals will appear.

Glue Game

● **Crayola Crayons** and **Elmer's Glue-All.** To teach your younger brothers or sisters how to write their name, use a Crayola Crayon to write each child's name on a separate piece of paper, and then trace over the letters using Elmer's Glue-All. When the glue dries, the children can use their fingers to trace along the tactile letters of their names, making it easier to understand the shapes of the letters.

Sealant

● **Aqua Net Hair Spray.** When sprayed on a chalk drawing, Aqua Net Hair Spray acts as a fixative, preventing art work from fading.

Storage

● **Clorox Bleach jug.** To make a carrier for small toys and crayons, with adult supervision, use a knife to cut a hole in the side of an empty, clean Clorox Bleach jug opposite the handle.

● **Cool Whip tub.** Keep crayons in a clean, empty Cool Whip canister.

● **Huggies Baby Wipes box.** Store crayons inside a clean, empty Huggies Baby Wipes box.

● **Kleenex Tissues box.** A decorative Kleenex Tissues box, when empty, makes an excellent container for storing crayons.

● **Cascade.** To clean crayon marks from walls, have an adult make a paste from a teaspoon of Cascade and a teaspoon of water, smear the paste over the crayon marks, wait ten minutes, and then wipe clean with a damp cloth.

● **Colgate Toothpaste.** Squeeze a dab of Colgate toothpaste on crayon marks on a wall and scrub. The mild abrasives in the toothpaste remove the crayon marks from the wall.

● **Conair Pro Styler 1600 Hair Dryer** and **Bounty Paper Towels.** To get crayon marks off walls, have an adult use a hair dryer set on warm to melt the wax, and then wipe the crayon marks off with a Bounty Paper Towel.

● **Huggies Baby Wipes.** Use Huggies Baby Wipes to wipe crayon marks off the walls and floors.

● **WD-40, Bounty Paper Towels,** and **Dawn Dishwashing Liquid.** Have an adult spray WD-40 over the crayon marks and wipe clean with a Bounty Paper Towel. To clean any residue left on the wall from the WD-40, just wipe clean with some soapy water made with a few drops of Dawn Dishwashing Liquid.

● **Pringles can** and **Con-Tact Paper.** Use an empty Pringles can decorated with Con-Tact paper.

● **Ziploc Storage Bags.** Keep a few crayons in a Ziploc Storage Bag for trips so you always have something to do in restaurants or during car trips.

Sun Catcher

● **Crayola Crayons** and **Reynolds Cut-Rite Wax Paper.** Using a small pencil sharpener, shave Crayola Crayons onto a sheet of Reynolds Cut-Rite Wax Paper. Fold the wax paper in half, covering all the shavings. With adult supervision, press with a warm iron until the crayon shavings melt. When cool, thread string through the top of the wax paper and hang in a window.

STRANGE FACTS

● In an episode of *The Simpsons*, a medical experiment reveals that Homer has a crayon lodged in his brain. Homer recalls that as a child he shoved an entire box of crayons up his nose and sneezed all of them out except for one.

● The White Cliffs of Dover in England are made from chalk.

● Calcium carbonate, the main ingredient in chalk, is the key ingredient in toothpaste (such as Colgate) and antacid tablets (such as Tums).

● In 1903, Binney & Smith made the first box of Crayola Crayons, costing a nickel and containing eight colors: red, orange, yellow, green, blue, violet, brown, and black.

● Red and black are the most popular crayon colors, mostly because children tend to use them for outlining.

● In 2003, to mark the one hundredth birthday of Crayola Crayons, consumers named four news colors (Inch Worm, Jazzberry Jam, Mango Tango, and Wild Blue Yonder) and voted four old colors out of the box of 120 Crayola Crayons (Blizzard Blue, Magic Mint, Mulberry, and Teal Blue).

● *Harold and the Purple Crayon* books by Crockett Johnson feature a boy named Harold who draws himself into adventures with his purple crayon.

Decorations

Artwork
● **Oral-B Dental Floss.** Use Oral-B Dental Floss, which is stronger and more durable than ordinary string, to hang pictures, sun catchers, or wind chimes.

Bathroom Shower Decals
● **Con-Tact Paper.** Decorate shower doors with decals cut from Con-Tact Paper.

Bicycles
● **Con-Tact Paper.** Add racing stripes to a bicycle by cutting long strips from Con-Tact Paper and adhering to your bicycle.

Christmas Trees
● **Jet-Puffed Marshmallows.** String Jet-Puffed Marshmallows together with a needle and thread to form long chains and drape them around the tree.

● **Orville Redenbacher's Gourmet Popping Corn.** Use a needle and thread to string popped Orville Redenbacher's Gourmet Popping Corn together. (Hint: Stale popcorn is easier to string than freshly popped popcorn.)

Christmas Lights
● **Forster Clothes Pins.** Help your parents hang Christmas lights by using Forster Clothes Pins to clip strings of lights to your house.

Helmets
● **Con-Tact Paper.** Make a bicycle or skateboard helmet easy to identify by adding shapes and designs cut from Con-Tact Paper.

Holiday Lanterns

● **Maxwell House Coffee.** Spray paint clean, empty Maxwell House Coffee cans with appropriate colors and designs for the holiday (a heart design on a red can for Valentine's Day, for instance), punch holes in the side of the can, fill the can halfway with sand, and (with adult supervision) place a lit candle inside to make attractive sidewalk decorations.

Party Streamers

● **Glad Trash Bags.** To make party streamers, cut a Glad Trash Bag into strips, starting from the open end and stopping two inches before you reach the bottom, and then hang in a doorway.

Skateboards

● **Con-Tact Paper.** Give a skateboard personality by cutting racing stripes or other funky shapes from Con-Tact Paper and adhere to the skateboard.

Snowflakes

● **Budweiser Beer** and **Epsom Salt.** With adult supervision, open a can of Budweiser Beer and let it sit undisturbed for twenty-four hours. Mix Epsom Salt with the flat beer until the beer can hold no more. Then apply the mixture to glass with a sponge. When it dries, the window will be frosted.

● **Con-Tact Paper.** Decorate windows with snowflakes cut from white Con-Tact Paper.

● **Mr. Coffee Filters.** Fold a Mr. Coffee filter many times and cut tiny holes. When opened, it will look like a snowflake.

Thanksgiving Turkey Centerpiece

● **Gold Medal Flour,** *USA Today,* and **Elmer's Glue-All.** Inflate a balloon to the size you want your turkey's body to be and tie a knot in the neck of the balloon. Mix one cup Gold Medal Flour with two-thirds cup water in a medium-size bowl to a thick-glue consistency. To thicken, add more flour. With adult supervision, use a pair of scissors to cut *USA Today* into strips approximately one to two inches in width. Dip each strip into the paste, gently pull it between your fingers to remove excess paste, and apply it to the balloon, leaving the knot exposed. Repeat until you have covered the balloon with three to four layers of newspaper strips. Set the mouth of the balloon on a paper cup and let dry completely. Pop the balloon and cover the hole with masking tape or more papier-mâché. Coat with brown paint. When dry, tape a one-inch wide ring of cardboard to the bottom to make a stand. Paint both sides of a sheet of poster board with fall colors (red, orange, yellow, and brown), allowing one side to dry before painting the second side. Let dry. Cut out a head, wings, tail feathers, and feet from the colorful poster board and glue into place on the body. You can also glue on buttons for eyes or decorate with colored rice (see page 109) or glitter. After the paint dries, coat with shellac.

Trays and Decorations

● **Reynolds Wrap.** Make decorative trays or holiday decorations by cutting cardboard into the desired shape and size and covering with Reynolds Wrap.

STRANGE FACTS

● In 1986, Gordon and Jasmine Geisbrecht opened The Outhouse, a restaurant in Winnipeg, Manitoba, decorated with toilet bowls around the dining room. Health inspectors shut down the restaurant for lacking sufficient bathrooms.

● In 1969, John Lennon and Yoko Ono celebrated their honeymoon by sitting in bed for seven consecutive days in a hotel suite at the Amsterdam Hilton decorated with posters that proclaimed "Bed Peace" and "Hair Peace."

● While serving as Vice President of the United States under President Gerald Ford, Nelson Rockefeller elaborately furnished and decorated the Vice President's mansion, but never lived there.

● In 1828, Joel Roberts Poinsett, the first United States Ambassador to Mexico, brought a Mexican plant with small yellow flowers surrounded by larger red and green leaves (*Euphorbia pulcherrima*) to the United States. The plant, called "flower of the blessed night" (because it resembled the Star of Bethlehem), was renamed in honor of Poinsett and quickly became a popular decoration for Christmas. If eaten, the leaves and stems of the poinsettia can cause abdominal cramps.

● Germans decorate Christmas trees with painted egg shells, people throughout the world decorate their trees with silver tinsel (to simulate icicles), and the Chinese decorate Christmas trees with paper lanterns.

● In New York City, Rockefeller Plaza employees decorate the Rockefeller Center Christmas Tree with 30,000 lights attached to five miles of wire.

Decoupage

Basic Decoupage

● **Elmer's Glue-All** and **Dixie Cups.** Cut out pictures from a glossy magazine or catalog (or cut out shapes from colored construction paper or decorative wrapping paper). Pour some Elmer's Glue-All into a Dixie Cup and using a paint brush, paint the glue on a piece of cardboard and place the cut-out pictures on the glued surface. Let dry. Paint a coat of glue over the finished piece of cardboard.

● **Con-Tact Paper** and **Elmer's Glue-All.** Cut out pictures from a glossy magazine or catalog (or cut out shapes from colored construction paper or decorative wrapping paper). Use just a small dab of glue to hold the cut-outs in place on a piece of cardboard (or whatever surface you wish to use). Use a piece of clear Con-Tact Paper, which has an adhesive back, to cover the artwork.

Other Tips

● **Campbell's Soup can.** Paint a clean, empty Campbell's Soup can with acrylic paint. Let dry. Then apply decoupage to the can to make a decorated pencil holder.

● **Clorox Bleach jug.** Apply decoupage to a clean, empty Clorox Bleach jug to make a decorated bank. Simply unscrew the cap to deposit coins inside.

● **Cool Whip tub.** Apply decoupage to a clean, empty Cool Whip container to make a decorative, resealable storage container.

● **Huggies Baby Wipes box.** Apply decoupage to a clean, empty Huggies Baby Wipes box to make a resealable storage container.

● **Maxwell House Coffee can.** Paint a clean, empty Maxwell House Coffee can with acrylic paint. Let dry. Then apply decoupage to the can and the plastic lid to make a resealable storage container.

● **Reynolds Wrap.** To add a touch of foil to your decoupage projects, cut shapes or confetti from Reynolds Wrap and glue into your artwork.

Sealant
● **Aqua Net Hair Spray.** Spray your finished decoupage project with a thin coat of Aqua Net Hair Spray to seal it and give it a glossy shine.

Tools
● **Campbell's Soup.** After you've glued the cut-outs in place, you can use an unopened can of Campbell's Soup as a rolling pin to smooth them out.

● **Forster Toothpicks.** If the edges of your cut-outs do not stick when you first glue them down, lift the edges carefully and apply a small amount of glue with a Forster Toothpick.

● **Q-Tips Cotton Swabs.** To wipe off excess glue in difficult corners, use a Q-Tips Cotton Swab dipped in water.

● **Scotch-Brite Heavy Duty Scrub Sponge.** Use a damp Scotch-Brite Heavy Duty Scrub Sponge to press down the edges of the cut-outs after you've glued them into place and to wipe off excess glue.

STRANGE FACTS

● The word *decoupage*, from the French *decouper*, meaning "to cut out," is the creative art of cutting out pictures and pasting them on furniture or home accessories to simulate painting.

● As early as the twelfth century, Chinese peasants created elaborate and detailed paper cutouts to decorate windows, lanterns, and gift boxes.

● In Eastern Siberia, ancient tombs of Siberian nomads were decorated with cutout felt figures and designs.

● Decoupage was originally known as poor man's art, enabling people who could not afford to hire an artist to decorate their furniture to achieve elegant effects by gluing on cut-outs covered with several coats of varnish or lacquer.

● Marie Antoinette, Madame de Pompadour, Lord Byron, Henri Matisse, Juan Gris, and Pablo Picasso created works of art using decoupage.

● The art of decoupage flourished in Europe during the eighteenth and nineteenth centuries, and highly skilled artisans perfected the art to such a fine degree that many elaborate decorations on boxes, trays, chests, and tables believed by experts to have been hand painted were later discovered to be decoupage cut outs.

● Materials that can be used for decoupage include magazines, catalogs, old books, wallpaper, gift wrapping paper, foil-covered paper, lace paper doilies, posters, travel brochures, and greeting cards.

Dolls and Puppets

Barbie Dolls

● **Johnson's Baby Powder.** The sticky, rubber legs on Barbie dolls often make dressing or undressing the dolls difficult. To make dressing Barbie dolls easier, sprinkle a small amount of Johnson's Baby Powder on the doll's legs. Dresses and pants will slide on or off easily.

● **Kingsford's Corn Starch.** Sprinkle a small amount of Kingsford's Corn Starch on the legs on Barbie dolls so the clothes slip on and off with greater ease, making dressing or undressing the dolls simple.

Dollhouses

● **Con-Tact Paper.** Wallpaper the rooms of a dollhouse with Con-Tact Paper, which makes excellent self-adhesive wallpaper in a wide variety of colors and snappy patterns.

Panty Hose Dolls

● **L'eggs Sheer Energy Panty Hose, Wilson Tennis Balls, Oral-B Dental Floss,** and **Uncle Ben's Converted Brand Rice.** Cut off the legs from a pair of clean, used L'eggs Sheer Energy Panty Hose. Slip a Wilson Tennis Ball into one foot to create the head, and then tie a piece of Oral-B Dental Floss around the neck to secure the head in place. Fill the leg of the panty hose with two cups Uncle Ben's Converted

Brand Rice to form the body, and then tie a knot in the open end to secure the body in place. To make arms and legs, cut sections from the other leg of the panty hose, tie one end closed with dental floss, fill with rice, and then secure the open end shut. Fold each section in half (to create two arms—or two legs—from one section) and secure in place with dental floss.

Paper Dolls
● **Con-Tact Paper.** To create paper dolls, cover magazine pictures with clear Con-Tact Paper and then cut them out.

Psychedelic Yarn Dolls
● **Kool-Aid.** Mix the contents of one packet Kool-Aid powdered mix with one cup warm water, soak white yarn in the brightly colored liquid for five minutes, and then rinse and let dry. Use the colored yarn to make yarn dolls. Wind the yarn lengthwise and loosely around a piece of cardboard measuring three inches by two inches. Slip a long piece of yarn under the wrapped yarn, slide it to the top end of the board, and tie a double knot. Slide a pair of scissors under the wrapped yarn to the bottom end of the board and cut the yarn. About an inch down from the top, tie a short piece of yarn around the strands of yarn to make the doll head, securing in place with a double knot. Lay the doll flat on a table. Count five strands of yarn on each side to make arms with fingers. Use a short piece of yarn to tie each arm half way up and trim.

Puppet Heads
● **Heinz Ketchup.** A clean, empty Heinz Ketchup bottle makes an excellent head for a puppet. Simply soak the bottle in warm water to peel off the label, hold the bottle upside down, and decorate to create a face.

Scarecrow
● **Clorox Bleach jug, L'eggs Sheer Energy Panty Hose, *USA Today*, Forster Clothes Pins,** and **Playtex Living Gloves.** Use a clean, empty Clorox Bleach jug for the head of

Barbie

Ruth Handler, inspired by her daughter, Barbara, who preferred playing with paper dolls that looked like adults, urged her husband, Elliot Handler, a cofounder of the Mattel toy company, to develop a doll with an adult body. Mattel's directors rejected the idea. During a trip to Europe, Handler bought an adult-figured German doll named Lilli, based on a popular comic strip character drawn by Reinhard Beuthin for die Bild-Zeitung. Mattel acquired the rights to the Lilli doll, which the company renamed Barbie, after Handler's daughter, Barbara. Mattel officially introduced Barbie at the New York International American Toy Fair on March 9, 1959 (Barbie's official birthday). Mattel fashion designer Charlotte Johnson designed Barbie's clothes, inspired by Paris fashions.

● If Barbie was an actual person, she would stand five feet, seven inches tall, and her measurements would be 36-18-33.

● Critics contend that Barbie's exaggerated proportions, uncharacteristic of most women, contribute to self-esteem, body image problems, and eating disorders in young girls.

● Barbie's full name is Barbara Millicent Roberts. Her friends include Ken Carson, Skipper, twins Tutti and Todd, Midge, Stacie, Kelly, Teresa, Christie, Steven, Kayla, and baby Krissy.

● On February 12, 2004, Mattel spokespeople announced that Barbie and Ken had split up after forty-three years of dating, saying in their press release that they "have decided to spend some time apart."

● Fashion designers who have designed clothing for Barbie include Calvin Klein, Donna Karan, Bob Mackie, Nicole Miller, Christian Dior, Escada, Anne Klein, Ralph Lauren, Donatella Versace, and Bill Blass.

● In 1989, the Barbie Liberation Organization bought hundreds of Teen Talk Barbie and the Talking Duke G.I. Joe dolls, and switched their voice circuitry (trimming circuit boards, moving a capacitor, and reengineering a switch), and then returned the altered dolls to the toy store shelves. Unsuspecting girls received modified Barbie dolls that said, "Vengeance is mine!" and "Eat lead, Cobra!" Boys got G.I. Joe action figures that said, "Let's plan our dream wedding!"

● In 2003, Saudi Arabia outlawed Barbie dolls.

a scarecrow by positioning the uncapped jug upside down on a broomstick and drawing a face on the jug with indelible marker. Pull the waist of a clean, used pair of L'eggs Sheer Energy Panty Hose over the base of the jug for hair. Stuff a long-sleeve shirt and a long pair of pants with crumpled up sheets of *USA Today* to make the body, which you can attach together using Forster Clothes Pins. Then stuff crumpled sheets of newspaper inside a pair of Playtex Living Gloves and attach the gloves to the ends of the shirt sleeves with clothes pins. Place a pair of shoes at the bottom of each pant leg or fill a pair of socks with crumpled newspaper and attach them to the bottom of each pant leg with clothes pins.

Stuffing
● **Glad Trash Bags.** With adult supervision, cut a Glad Trash Bag into strips and use it as waterproof stuffing for puppets or dolls.
● **Johnson & Johnson Cotton Balls.** Fill stuffed animals with Johnson & Johnson Cotton Balls.
● **Kleenex Tissues.** Use Kleenex Tissues to fill stuffed animals when sewing.

STRANGE FACTS
● Albert V, Duke of Bavaria between 1550 and 1579, owned the first dollhouse in recorded history. The dollhouse, a miniature copy of the duke's residence, became known as his "baby house."
● Dollhouses became popular in Germany, Holland, and England in the seventeenth and eighteenth centuries.
● In 1996, Mattel introduced the Cabbage Patch Snacktime doll, a Cabbage Patch doll with a motorized jaw that enabled it to mimic eating plastic cookies and other foods. When parents reported that the doll also ate children's hair and fingers, Mattel—facing an investigation by the Consumer Product Safety Commission—put warning labels on the dolls and admitted that it had failed to test the doll for possible hair entanglement. Finally, Mattel recalled the dolls and offered each consumer a forty-dollar refund.

Dough

Bread Modeling Dough
● **Wonder Bread, Elmer's Glue-All,** and **Reynolds Cut-Rite Wax Paper.** Remove the crust from several slices of Wonder Bread. Crinkle up the bread in a bowl and add one teaspoon Elmer's Glue-All for each slice of bread. Knead until the dough is no longer sticky. Model into whatever shape you desire and let dry on a sheet of Reynolds Cut-Rite Wax Paper. When dry, paint.

Chocolate Play Dough
● **Morton Salt, Gold Medal Flour, Hershey's Cocoa, McCormick Cream of Tartar, Wesson Vegetable Oil,** and **Ziploc Storage Bags.** With adult supervision, in a pot, bring two cups water and one-half cup Morton Salt to a boil. Stir in two cups Gold Medal Flour, one-third cup Hershey's Cocoa, two tablespoons McCormick Cream of Tartar, and two tablespoons Wesson Vegetable Oil. Mix well. Cook and stir over medium heat for three minutes (or until the mixture holds together). Let cool. Turn onto board or cookie sheet and knead to the proper consistency. Store in an airtight container or a Ziploc Storage Bag.

Coffee Play Dough
● **Maxwell House Coffee, Gold Medal Flour, Morton Salt,** and **Ziploc Storage Bags.** Mix one cup used Maxwell House Coffee Grounds, one-half cup cold, left-over Maxwell House coffee, one cup Gold Medal Flour, and one-half cup Morton Salt in a bowl until well blended. With your hands, knead the mixture on a floured surface to create a smooth dough. Store in an airtight container or Ziploc Storage Bag.

Kool-Aid Play Dough
● **Kool-Aid, Gold Medal Flour, Morton Salt, McCormick Alum, Wesson Vegetable Oil,** and **Ziploc Storage Bags.** Mix one packet of any unsweetened, colorful flavor of Kool-Aid with two cups water. Then add two cups Gold Medal Flour, one cup Morton Salt, two tablespoons McCormick Alum, and two tablespoons Wesson Vegetable Oil. Mix well. With adult supervision, cook and stir over medium heat for three minutes (or until the mixture holds together). Let cool. Turn onto board or cookie sheet and knead to the proper consistency. Store this fragrant, colorful dough in an airtight container or a Ziploc Storage Bag.

Peanut Butter Play Dough
● **Jif Peanut Butter, Carnation NonFat Dry Milk,** and **SueBee Honey.** Mix one cup Jif Peanut Butter (creamy), one-half cup Carnation NonFat Dry Milk, and one-quarter cup SueBee Honey. If the mixture is too sticky, add more powdered milk. Shape the dough as you please and, if desired, decorate with coconut, chopped peanuts, raisins, pretzels, or cereals. If used on a clean surface with clean hands, you can eat your creations.

Play Dough
● **McCormick Food Coloring, Gold Medal Flour, Morton Salt, McCormick Alum, Wesson Vegetable Oil,** and **Ziploc Storage Bags.** Add ten drops McCormick Food Coloring to two cups water. Then add two cups Gold Medal Flour, one cup Morton Salt, two tablespoons McCormick Alum, and two tablespoons Wesson

Vegetable Oil. Mix well. With adult supervision, cook and stir over medium heat for three minutes (or until the mixture holds together). Let cool. Turn onto board or cookie sheet and knead to a soft, pliable dough. Store in an airtight container or Ziploc Storage Bag.

Potato Play Dough

● **Betty Crocker Potato Buds.** With adult supervision, mix one cup Betty Crocker Potato Buds and two cups boiling water in a bowl. To make the dough thicker, add more potato flakes. To thin, add more boiling water. Let cool. You'll love playing with this tactile, gooey dough. If desired, add a few drops of food coloring.

Pumpkin-Pie Play Dough

● **McCormick Food Coloring, Gold Medal Flour, Morton Salt, McCormick Cream of Tartar, Wesson Vegetable Oil, McCormick Pumpkin Pie Spice,** and **Ziploc Storage Bags.** Add ten drops yellow McCormick Food Coloring and five drops red food coloring to four cups water. Then add five-and-a-half cups Gold Medal Flour, two cups Morton Salt, eight teaspoons McCormick Cream of Tartar, three-quarters cup Wesson Vegetable Oil, and one-and-a-half ounces McCormick Pumpkin Pie Spice. Mix well. With adult supervision, cook and stir over medium heat for three minutes (or until the mixture holds together). Let cool. Turn onto board or cookie sheet and knead the dough to a soft, pliable consistency. Store in an airtight container or Ziploc Storage Bag. Use cookie cutters, rolling pins, and small pie tins to make your own pretend pumpkin pies.

Rubbery Play Putty

● **Arm & Hammer Baking Soda, Kingsford's Corn Starch,** and **McCormick Food Coloring.** In a pot, mix two cups Arm & Hammer Baking Soda, one cup Kingsford's Corn Starch, and one-and-a-half cups water until smooth (to color the clay, add a few drops of McCormick Food Coloring). With adult supervision, boil over medium heat until the mixture thickens to the consistency of dough. Let cool. Knead into a smooth, pliable dough. After molding, let dry for eight hours. Paint and decorate, if desired.

Self-Hardening Play Dough

● **Elmer's Glue-All, Gold Medal Flour, Kingsford's Corn Starch, McCormick Food Coloring** (optional), and **Ziploc Storage Bags.** Mix equal parts Elmer's Glue-All, Gold Medal Flour, and Kingsford's Corn Starch. Mix and knead well until blended. If too dry, add more glue. If too moist, add more flour and cornstarch. Add McCormick Food Coloring if desired. The dough can be molded into any desired shape to create animals, figurines, ornaments, and jewelry. Let dry overnight. Paint and decorate, if desired.

Snow Dough

● **Gold Medal Flour, Morton Salt, McCormick Alum, Wesson Vegetable Oil,** and **Ziploc Storage Bags.** Mix two cups Gold Medal Flour, one cup Morton Salt, two tablespoons McCormick Alum, two tablespoons Wesson Vegetable Oil, and two cups water. To make the Snow Dough whiter, add three teaspoons white tempera paint. Mix well. With adult supervision, cook and stir over medium heat for three minutes (or until the mixture holds together). Let cool. Turn onto a board or cookie sheet and knead the dough into a soft, pliable consistency. If desired, add silver glitter and knead thoroughly until the dough sparkles like snow. Store in an airtight container or Ziploc Storage Bag.

STRANGE FACTS

● If rolled together, all the Play-Doh manufactured since it was invented in 1956 would make a ball weighing more than 700 million pounds.

● If all the Play-Doh made since 1956 was squeezed through a Play-Doh Fun Factory, it would make a snake that would wrap around the earth nearly three hundred times.

● Kids eat more Play-Doh than crayons, finger paint, and white paste combined.

● The Play-Doh boy, pictured on every can of Play-Doh, is named Play-Doh Pete and was created in 1960.

● In 1955, brothers Noah and Joseph McVicker of Cincinnati,

Ohio, having invented a doughy wallpaper cleaner, realized that their invention doubled as an excellent non-toxic modeling compound for children. They cleverly named their cream-colored modeling dough "Play-Doh" and tested it in nursery schools, kindergartens, and elementary schools in Cincinnati.

● In 1940, the United States War Production Board asked General Electric to synthesize an inexpensive substitute for rubber. Three years later James Wright, a company engineer assigned to the project in New Haven, Connecticut, combined boric acid and silicone oil in a test tube and developed a pliant, bouncing compound dubbed "nutty putty" with no real advantages over synthetic rubber.

● In 1949, Paul Hodgson, a former advertising copywriter writing the catalog for the Block Shop toy store in New Haven, happened to witness a demonstration of the "nutty putty" at a party. He bought 21 pounds of the putty for $147, hired a Yale student to separate it into half-ounce balls, and marketed the putty inside colored plastic eggs as Silly Putty. When it outsold every other item in his store, Hodgson mass-produced Silly Putty as "the toy with one moving part," selling up to three hundred eggs a day.

● The astronauts on *Apollo 8* played with Silly Putty during their flight and used it to keep tools from floating around in zero gravity.

● Americans buy more than two million eggs of Silly Putty every year.

● In 2000, the Smithsonian Institution put two early eggs of Silly Putty on exhibit.

Finger Paints

● **Betty Crocker Frosting.** Scoop a few spoonfuls of Betty Crocker chocolate and vanilla frostings into small bowls and use as finger paint.

● **Carnation Condensed Milk** and **McCormick Food Coloring.** Mix one-quarter cup Carnation Condensed Milk with your choice of a few drops of McCormick Food Coloring to make a great glossy finger paint.

● **Carnation Nonfat Dry Milk** and **McCormick Food Coloring.** Mix three cups Carnation Nonfat Dry Milk and one cup water until it is the consistency of paint. Blend in McCormick Food Coloring to make the desired hue. Thin the paint by adding more water; thicken the paint by adding more powdered milk.

● **Cool Whip** and **McCormick Food Coloring** (or **Kool-Aid**). Scoop Cool Whip into several bowls and mix the contents of each bowl with a different color McCormick Food Coloring (or with various flavors of unsweetened Kool-Aid powder mix).

● **Crisco All-Vegetable Shortening** and **McCormick Food Coloring.** Mix a few tablespoons of Crisco All-Vegetable Shortening with a few drops of McCormick Food Coloring in a bowl to make finger paint.

● **Dannon Yogurt** and **McCormick Food Coloring.** Mix Dannon Plain Yogurt with McCormick Food Coloring right in the container and let young children finger paint with it, without having to worry about them eating real paint. Or use various fruit-flavored yogurts as strawberry (pink), blueberry (blue), and lemon (yellow) finger paints.

● **French's Mustard** and **Heinz Ketchup.** In a pinch, you can finger paint by simply squeezing French's Mustard and Heinz Ketchup onto the glossy side of a sheet of finger-paint paper or butcher paper.

● **Gillette Foamy Shaving Cream** and **McCormick Food Coloring.** In small bowls, mix Gillette Foamy Shaving Cream with a few drops of McCormick Food Coloring. You can paint with Gillette Foamy on a kitchen table, vinyl tablecloth, or—for easy cleanup—in the bathtub. On a sunny day, get into your bathing suit and finger paint with shaving cream on a plastic table in the backyard. When you're done, just hose the table and yourself clean.

● **Gold Medal Flour, McCormick Food Coloring,** and **20 Mule Team Borax** (optional). Mix one-half cup Gold Medal Flour with one-half cup water to make a paste. Add another one-and-a-half cups water and, with adult supervision, cook over low heat, stirring constantly, until the mixture turns thick and clear. Remove from heat and let cool. If desired, add one tablespoon glycerin (available at the drug store) if you wish to slow the drying process. If necessary, thin the paint by adding more water. Add McCormick Food Coloring to make desired hue. To store in airtight containers, add one teaspoon 20 Mule Team Borax and mix well.

(Omit borax if finger paint is to be used by small children; borax can be toxic if swallowed.)

● **Ivory Snow, Sta-Flo Liquid Starch,** and **McCormick Food Coloring.** Blend one-half cup Ivory Snow (powder) and two tablespoons of Sta-Flo Liquid Starch with an eggbeater or a whisk in a mixing bowl, until it reaches the consistency of whipped cream. Pour the mixture into different jars, add a few drops of a different color McCormick Food Coloring into each jar, and stir well. Finger

● **Colgate Toothpaste.** You can use a dollop of Colgate Toothpaste as if it were liquid soap to help remove finger paint from hands.

● **Gillette Foamy Shaving Cream.** If you don't have any soap or dishwashing liquid, you can clean finger paint from hands with a dollop of Gillette Foamy Shaving Cream and running water. Shaving cream can also be used to clean paint from carpet. Simply spray on some foam, scrub with a wet scrub brush, and then rinse with a wet cloth to blot up the extra foam.

● **Huggies Baby Wipes.** Simply wipe off the paint from hands with Huggies Baby Wipes, which can also clean paint from walls and carpet.

● **Morton Salt.** To clean paint from carpet, pour a mountain of Morton Salt to cover the stain, and then watch the salt absorb the paint. Then sweep up the salt. Wash with soapy water and blot.

● **Windex.** In a pinch, Windex cleans paint from carpets. Simply spray and blot up.

paint with the soapy paint on sheets of brown paper. If the soapsuds thicken, add more starch and stir well. Give the finished artwork ample time to dry.

● **Jell-O.** Mix the powdered mix from a three-ounce box of a colorful flavor of Jell-O powder with a small amount of warm water to achieve the consistency of toothpaste. For best results, use this fragrant, gritty, and edible finger paint on the glossy side of finger-paint paper or butcher paper.

● **Jell-O** and **Kingsford's Corn Starch.** Dissolve one packet Jell-O powder in one-quarter cup hot water and set aside. In a pot, mix one-half cup Kingsford's Corn Starch and three-quarters cup water to make a smooth paste. With adult supervision, pour two cups boiling water into the cornstarch solution while stirring. Stir over medium heat until the mixture boils and goes clear. Remove from the heat, pour into the Jell-O solution, and stir well. Let cool. Repeat with different flavors of Jell-O to make different colors of finger paint. Store in an airtight container or clean baby food jars.

● **Jell-O Instant Vanilla Pudding** and **McCormick Food Coloring.** Using a whisk, beat the pudding mix (from a one-ounce box) into two cups cold fat-free milk in a bowl for two minutes. Immediately pour equal amounts of the mixture into several small bowls. Within five minutes, the pudding will soft-set. Add McCormick Food Coloring to each bowl of pudding to achieve the desired color and finger paint with this delicious concoction.

● **Kingsford's Corn Starch, McCormick Food Coloring, Glycerin** (optional), and **Listerine** (optional). With adult supervision, mix one-quarter cup Kingsford's Corn Starch with two cups cold water, boil until thick, pour into small containers, and color with McCormick Food Coloring. If desired, add one tablespoon glycerin (available at the drug store) if you wish to slow the drying process. To store in airtight containers, first add two teaspoons Listerine as a preservative and mix well.

● **Kool-Aid, Gold Medal Flour, Morton Salt,** and **Wesson Corn Oil.** In a large bowl, mix one packet unsweetened Kool-Aid, one cup Gold Medal Flour, one-quarter cup Morton Salt, and one-and-a-half tablespoons Wesson Corn Oil. With adult supervision, add three cups boiling water and stir well. Repeat with different flavors of Kool-Aid to make a variety of colors.

● **Knox Gelatin, Kingsford's Corn Starch, C&H Sugar, Ivory Dishwashing Liquid,** and **McCormick Food Coloring.** Dissolve one packet powdered, unflavored Knox Gelatin in one-quarter cup hot water and set aside. In a pot, mix one-half cup Kingsford's Corn Starch, three tablespoons C&H Sugar, and one-and-three-quarters cups cold water, stirring until cloudy and smooth. With adult supervision, cook the mixture over a medium-high heat, stirring constantly. When the mixture becomes clear and thick, reduce the heat and pour in the gelatin mixture and one-quarter cup Ivory Dishwashing Liquid. Mix until smooth, and then let cool. Pour equal amounts of the mixture into small bowls or baby food jars. Add several drops of McCormick Food Coloring to each bowl or jar and mix well. Let cool. Store the finger paints in airtight jars.

● **Kraft Handi-Snacks Vanilla Pudding** and **McCormick Food Coloring.** Open each one of the four cups of pudding, add a few drops of a different color of McCormick Food Coloring to each cup, and stir well with a spoon. Then use as finger paint.

● **Reddi-wip** and **McCormick Food Coloring.** Tape a sheet of finger-paint paper or butcher paper (glossy side up) to a tabletop. Shake the can of Reddi-wip, spray a few small mounds of whipped cream on the paper, and add a few drops of a different colored food coloring to each mound. Finger paint away!

STRANGE FACTS

● As early as 30,000 B.C.E., Paleolithic Europeans and Africans mixed animal fats with clay pigments to make paint, which they finger painted on mud and rock cave walls.

● Chinese artists created finger paintings as early as 750 C.E.

● Finger painting entered its golden age in China during the Qing Dynasty (1644–1911 C.E.), and Chinese artist Gao Qipei (1672–1734) is generally considered the first genuine finger painter.

● Finger painting is used as a form of therapy for the mentally ill, allowing them to express their feelings easily.

Flowers

Coloring Cut Flowers

● **McCormick Food Coloring.** Mix a few drops of McCormick Food Coloring into warm water and place the flower stems in the solution overnight. The stems will absorb the colors by morning, revealing intriguing designs on the flower petals in different colors.

● **Mrs. Stewart's Liquid Bluing.** Freshly cut carnations placed in a vase with a high content of Mrs. Stewart's Liquid Bluing in the water will by osmosis quickly carry the blue color into the tips of the petals.

Dry Flowers

● **Aqua Net Hair Spray.** Brighten and preserve dried flower arrangements or grapevine wreaths by spraying them with Aqua Net Hair Spray, giving the flowers a slight shine.

● **L'eggs Sheer Energy Panty Hose** and **Forster Clothes Pins.** To dry flowers, remove most of the leaves from the flower stems to improve air circulation, reduce the risk of mildew, and expedite the drying process. With adult supervision, remove the thorns from roses with a sharp pair of scissors to avoid pricking yourself. Cut the stems to different lengths. Bundle together a group of six stems loosely with a loop of nylon cut from a leg of a pair of clean, used L'eggs Sheer Energy Panty Hose, staggering the flower heads so they do not touch each other. (As the stems dry and shrink, the nylon loop will contract, holding the bunch together.) String a line of rope or twine tautly across a dry, warm, airy room. Attach the bundled flowers upside down to the indoor clothesline with Forster Clothes Pins, making sure the flowers do not touch anything. Do not hang the flowers in direct sunlight, which will fade the colors. The faster the plant material dries, the more color the flowers, leaves, and stems will retain. (Strung flowers also make excellent decorations.)

Flower Arrangement
● **Scotch Tape.** Keep long-stemmed flowers standing upright in a vase by crisscrossing Scotch Tape across the mouth of the vase.

Flower Extenders
● **Glad Drinking Straws.** To elongate flower stems that are too short for a vase, insert the flower stem into a Glad Drinking Straw cut to whatever length you need.

Flower Power
● **Alka-Seltzer.** Prolong the life of cut flowers in a vase by dropping in two Alka-Seltzer tablets per quart of water.

● **Arm & Hammer Baking Soda.** Cut flowers last longer if you add one teaspoon Arm & Hammer Baking Soda per quart of water in the vase.

● **Bounty Paper Towels.** To revitalize wilted flowers, add a few ice cubes to the vase and cover the flowers with a sheet of Bounty Paper Towels dampened with cold water.

● **Clorox Bleach.** Adding one-quarter teaspoon Clorox Bleach to each quart of water used in a vase of cut flowers prolongs the life of the flowers by killing the harmful bacteria in the water.

● **Crayola Crayons.** To seal cut flowers, with adult supervision carefully unwrap a green Crayola Crayon, place it in a coffee cup, and heat it in the microwave oven until the wax melts. Dip the end of the stem of a cut flower into the hot wax. The green wax seals the stem and keeps the flower looking fresh longer.

● **Heinz White Vinegar** and **C&H Sugar.** Extend the life of cut flowers by dissolving two tablespoons Heinz White Vinegar and three tablespoons C&H Sugar per quart of warm water in a vase, making sure the stems are covered by three to four inches of the prepared water. The vinegar inhibits bacterial growth while the sugar feeds the plants.

● **Listerine.** Adding one-half teaspoon Listerine (original or Cool Mint) per quart of water in a vase extends the life of cut flowers. The antiseptic inhibits the growth of harmful bacteria.

● **Morton Salt.** Prolong the life of freshly cut flowers by adding a pinch of Morton Salt to the water in the vase. Salt slows the growth of harmful bacteria.

● **Oral-B Dental Floss.** To prevent the stems of primroses from bending over in a vase, use a piece of Oral-B Dental Floss to gently tie the stems together just beneath the flowers.

● **7-Up.** Filling a vase of cut flowers with one part 7-Up to two parts water makes the flowers last longer and look healthier. The high sugar content in the Uncola nourishes the plants.

Preserved Flowers

● **20 Mule Team Borax, Albers Corn Meal,** and **Tupperware.**
To preserve flowers, mix one part 20 Mule Team Borax and two parts Albers Corn Meal. Fill the bottom inch of an empty airtight Tupperware canister with the mixture. Place the flower on the mixture, and then gently cover the flower with more mixture, being careful not to crush the flower or distort the petals. Flowers with a lot of overlapping petals, such as roses and carnations, are best treated by sprinkling the mixture directly into the blossoms before placing them into the canister. Seal the canister and store at room temperature in a dry place for seven to ten days. When the flowers are dried, pour off the mixture and dust the flowers with a soft artist's brush. The borax and corn meal remove the moisture from blossoms and leaves, preventing the wilting that would normally result.

Pressed Flowers

● **Mr. Coffee Filters.** To press flowers dry, place a Mr. Coffee Filter flat on a hardcover book, lay a flat flower or a bud on the filter, lay a second coffee filter flat on top of the flower, and then place

several hardcover books on top. Let set for one week, and then frame
the pressed flower.

Vases
● **Gatorade bottle.** Make a vase by removing the label from a
clean, empty Gatorade bottle, fill one-quarter of the way with marbles
(to weight down the bottle), fill half way with water, and fill with
flowers.
● **Pampers.** With adult supervision, use a pair of scissors
to carefully cut open a Pampers disposable diaper. Pour the
superabsorbent polymer flakes from the diaper into a vase and add
water. The polymer flakes absorb three hundred times their weight in
water, giving the vase a decorative look. Then add the flowers to the
vase.

Winter Flowers
● **Johnson & Johnson Cotton Balls, Parsons' Ammonia**, and
Glad Trash Bags. To make flowers bloom in winter, prune some
twigs or branches of forsythia, crab apple, hawthorn, lilac, or other
flowering trees and shrubs. With adult supervision, put the stems in a
bucket of warm water, and then drop in a Johnson & Johnson Cotton
Ball soaked with Parsons' Ammonia. Put the bucket and branches in a
Glad Trash Bag and seal securely with a twist tie. The ammonia fumes
will force blooms on the branches.

STRANGE FACTS
● Carnations, daylilies, marigolds, nasturtiums, pansies, roses, and
violets are all edible flowers.
● Fear of flowers is called anthophobia.
● The flowers of chocolate cosmos (*Cosmos atrosanguineus*) smell like
cocoa.
● Since the early seventeenth century, Dutch tulip hybridizers have
attempted to breed a pure black tulip, but none have succeeded.
● In 1850, French novelist Alexander Dumas, author of *The Count
of Monte Cristo, The Three Musketeers*, and *The Man in the Iron Mask*,

published his novel *The Black Tulip*, a romantic tale that created popular fervor for the fictional black tulip.

● In Lewis Carroll's 1872 children's book *Through the Looking Glass*, when Alice asks why she has never heard flowers talk in other gardens, the Tiger-lily replies, "In most gardens they make the beds too soft— so that the flowers are always asleep."

● The slogan "Say it with flowers," used by the Society of American florists, was coined by Patrick O'Keefe in the December 15, 1917, issue of *Florists' Exchange*.

● "Poppies! Poppies will make them sleep!" chants the Wicked Witch of the West in the 1939 movie classic *The Wizard of Oz*, as she casts a spell over a field of flowers. In the book *The Wonderful Wizard of Oz*, written by L. Frank Baum in 1900, thousands of field mice pull the Cowardly Lion out of the Deadly Poppy Field. In the movie, Glinda— the Good Witch of the North—saves Dorothy, Toto, and the Lion by smothering the deadly scent of the poppies with snow.

● The Kingston Trio recorded the 1962 hit song "Where Have All the Flowers Gone?" written by folk singer Pete Seeger. Seeger had been inspired by three lines from a Ukrainian folk song that he read in the novel *And Quiet Flows the Don* by Mikhail Sholokhov. The lines were: "Where are the flowers? The girls have plucked them. Where are the girls? They've all taken husbands. Where are the men? They're all in the army."

Food Fun

Birthday Cake
● **Oral-B Dental Floss.** To cut a birthday cake into neat slices, simply cut off a long piece of dental floss as if you were going to floss your teeth, and then press it into the cake, release one end, and pull the floss through the cake. Repeat. Many fine restaurants use this technique to slice their cakes—especially cheesecake.

Caramel Corn
● **Orville Redenbacher's Gourmet Popping Corn, C&H Brown Sugar, Land O Lakes Butter, Karo Light Corn Syrup, Morton Salt, Arm & Hammer Baking Soda** and **Tupperware** or **Ziploc Storage Bags.** With adult supervision, air-pop enough Orville Redenbacher's Gourmet Popping Corn to make four quarts of popcorn. Preheat the oven to 200 degrees Fahrenheit. Divide the popcorn between two ungreased rectangular pans, 13 x 9 x 2 inches. Combine one cup C&H Brown Sugar (packed), one-half cup Land O Lakes Butter, one-quarter cup Karo Light Corn Syrup, and one-half teaspoon Morton Salt in a saucepan. Heat over medium heat, stirring occasionally, until the mixture starts bubbling around the edges. Cook for five minutes, stirring occasionally. Remove from the heat and blend in one-half teaspoon Arm & Hammer Baking Soda. Pour the syrup over the popped corn, stirring until coated thoroughly. Bake for one hour, stirring every fifteen minutes. Remove from the heat and let cool. When cool, break apart and store in an airtight Tupperware container or a Ziploc Storage Bag.

Cheerios Treats
● **Blue Bonnet Margarine, Jet-Puffed Miniature Marshmallows, Jif Peanut Butter,** and **Cheerios.** With

adult supervision, grease a rectangular pan, 13 x 9 x 2 inches. Microwave three tablespoons Blue Bonnet Margarine in a large microwaveable bowl on high for 45 seconds, or until melted. Add one package Jet-Puffed Miniature Marshmallows (six cups) or forty large marshmallows. Toss to coat with margarine. Microwave on high for 45 seconds, stir, and then microwave for another 45 seconds (or until smooth when stirred). Stir in one-half cup smooth or crunchy Jif Peanut Butter. Immediately add five cups Cheerios cereal. Mix until well coated. Using a greased spatula or wax paper, press the mixture into the prepared pan. Cool. Cut into squares. Makes about 24. (You can also mix one cup M&M's Chocolate Candies or one cup Sun-Maid Raisins and one-half cup dry-roasted Planters Peanuts along with the cereal; add to warm marshmallow-peanut mixture.)

Coffee-Can Bread

● **Gold Medal All-Purpose Flour, Fleischman's Active Dry Yeast, Land O Lakes Butter, C&H Sugar, Morton Salt, Crisco All-Vegetable Shortening,** and **Maxwell House Coffee can.** Mix one cup Gold Medal All-Purpose Flour with half the contents of one package Fleischman's Active Dry Yeast. In a saucepan, mix together one-quarter cup water, one-quarter cup milk, one-quarter cup Land O Lakes Butter, one ounce C&H Sugar, and one-half teaspoon Morton Salt. With adult supervision, stir over low heat until the butter melts, let cool for five minutes, and then pour in the bowl of flour. Beat until smooth. Add one more cup flour and one slightly beaten egg and mix well. Knead on a floured board. Use the Crisco All-Vegetable Shortening to lightly grease the inside of the Maxwell House Coffee can, stuff the dough into the can, and cover with the plastic lid. Set in a warm spot (roughly 85 degrees Fahrenheit) to allow the dough to rise. When the dough rises about one inch from the top of the can (usually after one hour), remove the plastic lid, preheat the oven to 375 degrees Fahrenheit, place the dough-filled coffee can in the oven, and bake for 35 minutes (or until the bread appears well browned and sounds hollow when tapped). Remove from the oven, let cool in the can for ten minutes, and then turn out onto a rack to cool completely.

Cola Volcano

● **Tabasco Pepper Sauce** and **Coca-Cola.** To make a cola volcano, mix one or two drops Tabasco Pepper Sauce to a glass of Coca-Cola, stir well, add ice, and drink!

Cookies

● **Tang.** Add Tang to your cake and cookie mixes for an "orange zest."

Edible Glass

● **Land O Lakes Butter** and **C&H Sugar.** Butter a baking sheet with Land O Lakes Butter and place it in the refrigerator. Put one cup C&H Sugar in a heavy stainless steel or nonstick frying pan. With adult supervision, set the pan on a burner at low heat. Using a large wooden spoon, stir the sugar slowly as it heats up. The sugar will slowly turn tan, stick together in clumps, and begin melting into a pale brown liquid. Continue stirring until the sugar melts into a thick brown liquid. Pour the brown liquid into the cold baking sheet. Let cool. The melted sugar hardens into a sheet of edible sugar glass.

Gingerbread House

● **Jet-Puffed Marshmallow Creme, Honey Maid Graham Crackers,** and **M&M's Chocolate Candies.** Use a spoon to smooth Jet-Puffed Marshmallow Creme on one edge of a Honey Maid Graham Cracker. Place the sticky edge of the graham cracker against the one edge of a second graham cracker, using the marshmallow creme like mortar to build a house. Repeat for the other sides of the house. Break a graham cracker into whatever shapes you need to build the roof. Decorate the house by using the marshmallow creme as glue to adhere M&M's Chocolate Candies to the outside of your gingerbread house.

Homemade Yogurt

● **Dannon Yogurt.** Pour one quart half-and-half into a glass mixing bowl. With adult supervision and using a cooking thermometer, heat the half-and-half in a microwave oven at fifty percent power for one minute at a time until the temperature of the half-and-half reaches 180 degrees Fahrenheit. (Use the spoon to stir the liquid between time breaks to prevent scalding and skim off any film from the surface.) Remove from the microwave and let cool to about 115 degrees Fahrenheit.

Add three tablespoons Dannon Plain Yogurt, mix well, pour into a clean, empty glass jar, and seal the lid tightly. Place the warm jar inside an insulated picnic cooler, close the lid, and let sit undisturbed for eight hours. Refrigerate when ready. You've made plain yogurt. If you wish, add vanilla extract, strawberries, peaches, or raspberries to taste. Three tablespoons of yogurt from this batch can be used to start a new batch, ideally within five days.

Ice Cream

● **Jell-O Instant Pudding, Maxwell House Coffee,** and **Morton Rock Salt.** Empty the contents of the Jell-O Instant Pudding mix into a large mixing bowl. Add three cups milk (according to the directions on the back of the box) and mix well using a whisk. Pour the pudding solution into a small, clean Maxwell House coffee can (11.5 ounce). Secure the plastic lid in place and use electrical tape to make the lid watertight. Place the small coffee can into a large Maxwell House Coffee can (34.5 ounce). Fill the rest of the can with ice up to the top of the small can. Fill the rest of the space with Morton Rock Salt. Secure the plastic lid in place and use electrical tape to make the lid watertight. Take the can outside and roll it back and forth across the lawn or patio for fifteen minutes. Bring the can back inside, peel the tape from the lid of the large can, pour out the melted ice and salt, and refill with fresh ice and fresh salt. Secure the lid in place again and roll the can outside for another fifteen minutes.

Bring the can back inside, peel off the tape from the large can, pour out the melted ice and salt, and wash off the small can with tap water from the sink. Dry the can. Store in the freezer for twelve hours. Peel off the tape from the small can, remove the lid, and scoop the contents into bowls.

Ice Cream Cone Drip-Stopper
● **Jet-Puffed Marshmallows.** Prevent ice cream cone drips by stuffing a Jet-Puffed Marshmallow in the bottom of a sugar cone.

Mashed Potatoes in Technicolor
● **McCormick Food Coloring.** Make colorful mashed potatoes by adding a few drops of McCormick Food Coloring to the mashed potatoes to make festive holiday food (green for St. Patrick's Day, orange for Halloween, and red for Valentine's Day).

Party Favors
● **Mr. Coffee Filters.** Place candy in the middle of a Mr. Coffee Filter and tie the sides together with a ribbon.

Rock Candy
● **C&H Sugar** and **Kool-Aid.** With adult supervision, to make colorful rock candy, fill a clean, empty mayonnaise jar with one-quarter cup boiling water and slowly add two cups C&H Sugar and one packet Kool-Aid (whatever flavor you like). Stir well. Attach a clean nail to one end of a string and a pencil to the other end of the string. Place the pencil on the mouth of the jar so the nail hangs down into the thick sugar water without touching the bottom of the jar. Place the jar in a warm place and let stand for a few days. As the water evaporates, colorful rocklike sugar crystals form on the string.

Snow Cones
● **Country Time Lemonade.** To make lemon-flavored snow cones, sprinkle Country Time Lemonade (just the powder) on a bowl full of newly fallen snow and eat with a spoon.
● **Tang.** To make tangy orange snow cones, fill a bowl with newly

fallen snow, sprinkle Tang (just the powder) on top of it, and dig in with a spoon.

Soft Drinks
● **Canada Dry Club Soda.** Make inexpensive soft drinks by adding Canada Dry to fruit juice for a low-cost and healthy beverage.

Spicy Popcorn
● **Tabasco Pepper Sauce** and **Orville Redenbacher's Gourmet Popping Corn.** With adult supervision, make spicy popcorn by adding a few drops of Tabasco Pepper Sauce to the cooking oil before adding the popcorn kernels.

STRANGE FACTS
● The shopping cart was invented by businessman Sylvan Nathan Goldman, who introduced his invention on June 4, 1937, in the Piggly-Wiggly supermarket chain he owned in Oklahoma City. When customers refused to use the new invention, Goldman hired models to push shopping carts around the store to demonstrate their usefulness. Goldman quickly became a multimillionaire by collecting a royalty on every shopping cart manufactured in the United States (until his patents expired).

● The word *gourmand* means "a connoisseur of good food who tends to overeat."

● In 1964, Kellogg and the Post Cereal Company, eager to cash in on the concept of freeze-dried foods popularized by the space program, added freeze-dried fruits to their corn flake cereals. However, consumers quickly discovered that the pieces of freeze-dried fruit in the corn flakes had to soak in milk for nearly ten minutes before they reconstituted, by which time the corn flakes were soggy and unappetizing.

● In his book, *The Food Revolution,* John Robbins, son of Baskin-Robbins cofounder Irv Robbins, tells that his family had "an ice cream cone-shaped swimming pool, our cats were named after ice cream flavors, and I sometimes ate ice cream for breakfast."

Games

Alpha-Bits Word Search
● **Post Alpha-Bits.** The first player randomly selects ten pieces
of the letter-shaped cereal from a box of Post Alpha-Bits and writes
down how many words he or she can make out of those ten letters in
three minutes. Each in turn, the other players select ten pieces and do
the same. Score one point for a two-letter word, five points for a three-
letter word, ten points for a four-letter word, fifteen points for five-
letter word, twenty points for a six-letter word, twenty-five points for a
seven-letter word, thirty points for an eight-letter word, forty points for
a nine-letter word, and one hundred points for a ten-letter word.

Basket Tennis
● **Wilson Tennis Balls** and **Maxwell House Coffee can.**
Remove the bottom from an empty Maxwell House Coffee can and
nail the can above the garage door. Use a Wilson Tennis Ball to play
basketball.

Beanbag Toss
● **Campbell's Soup cans.** Stack six clean, empty Campbell's
Soup cans on top of each other with three cans on the bottom, two
cans in the middle, and one can on top. Toss beanbags (see page 129)
to knock down the cans.
● **Hula Hoop.** Lay a Hula Hoop on the ground and place a second
Hula Hoop on the ground several feet away. Stand inside the second
hoop, and see how many beanbags (see page 129) you can toss into the
first hoop.
● **Maxwell House Coffee can.** Place a clean, empty Maxwell
House Coffee can on the ground, stand back several feet, and see how
many beanbags (see page 129) you can toss into the can.

Bowling

● **Campbell's Soup** and **Dixie Cups** (or **Coca-Cola bottles**). Roll an unopened Campbell's Soup can as an impromptu bowling ball to knock down Dixie Cups or Coca-Cola bottles.

● **Gatorade bottles** and **Con-Tact Paper.** Use ten clean, empty Gatorade bottles as bowling pins. Decorate the bottles with Con-Tact Paper and use a rubber ball to bowl.

● **Maxwell House Coffee** and **Scotch Packaging Tape.** Can't find an appropriate ball? Roll an unopened Maxwell House Coffee can at your homemade bowling pins (or fill a clean, empty Maxwell House coffee can halfway with sand and seal the lid closed with Scotch Packaging Tape).

Cards

● **Forster Clothes Pins.** To help small children play cards, use a Forster Clothes Pin to clip a hand of playing cards together so the kids can hold them more easily.

● **Gold Medal Flour.** To clean a deck of playing cards, place the deck of cards in a paper bag, add four tablespoons Gold Medal Flour, and shake briskly. Remove the cards from the bag and wipe clean.

● **Kingsford's Corn Starch.** Kingsford's Corn Starch works well for keeping an old deck of cards from sticking together. Simply place the cards in a paper bag, add four tablespoons Kingsford's Corn Starch, and shake well. Remove the cards and wipe clean.

Chalk Games

● **Crayola Chalk.** Draw on the concrete floor in the garage or patio with Crayola Chalk to create games (hopscotch, tic tac toe, dots), maps, and adventures.

Cheerios Air Hockey

● **Cheerios** and **Glad Plastic Straws.** All you need is one piece of Cheerios cereal, two Glad Plastic Straws, and a table. Each player gets one straw, the players stand at opposite ends of the table, and the Cheerios piece is placed in the center of the table. The players simultaneously blow through their straw at the Cheerios "puck" to blow it across the opposing player's edge of the table. The first player to score ten goals is the winner.

Croquet
● **Glad Drinking Straws.** On sunny days, when there's nothing to do around the house, make croquet wickets visible on the lawn by running the wickets through Glad Drinking Straws before sticking them in the ground.

Frisbee Golf
● **Frisbee.** On sunny days, when there's nothing to do around the house, designate a tee-off spot and choose a tree, pole, or other landmark as the hole. Toss a Frisbee toward the "hole," pick it up wherever it lands, and continue tossing until you hit the hole. Keep score. The player with the fewest tosses to hit all the holes wins.
● **Hula Hoop** and **Oral-B Dental Floss.** For more fun, use a long piece of Oral-B Dental Floss to hang a Hula Hoop from a tree branch to create more challenging "holes" for Frisbee Golf.

Marshmallow Golf
● **Jet-Puffed Marshmallows.** To play golf indoors, try using a Jet-Puffed Marshmallow as the ball. Use coffee mugs (or clean, empty Campbell's Soup cans) for the holes. If you don't have a golf club, you can putt with a yard stick, a mailing tube, or a plastic baseball bat. The player with the fewest strokes wins.

Marshmallow Obstacle Course
● **Jet-Puffed Marshmallows.** Have contestants run an obstacle course while balancing marshmallows on two spoons—one in each hand. Whoever drops a marshmallow must start again at the beginning.

Marshmallow Toss

● **Jet-Puffed Marshmallows.** Line up six beach pails in a vertical row and place a piece of masking tape two feet from the first pail. Standing behind the line of masking tape, toss a Jet-Puffed Marshmallow into each bucket, beginning with the closest one. The first person to toss a marshmallow into the farthest bucket wins.

Marshmallow Tower

● **Jet-Puffed Marshmallows.** See who can stack the most Jet-Puffed Marshmallows vertically on a table top.

Miniature Golf

● **Campbell's Soup cans.** On a sunny day, when there's nothing to do around the house, make a putting green in your backyard, by punching a few holes in the bottom of a few clean, empty Campbell's Soup cans and burying them in the grass. (The punched holes will allow water from rain or sprinklers to drain out.)

Pin the Tail on the Donkey

● **Post-it Notes.** Simply write each player's name on a strip cut from a Post-it Note. Instead of a picture of a donkey, you can use a full-page photograph from a magazine to play "Pin the Tail on Paris Hilton," "Pin the Nose on Britney Spears," or "Pin the Smile on Hilary Duff."

Sorting and Counting Game

● **M&M's.** Give smaller children a bag of M&M's Chocolate Candies and have them sort the M&M's by color. *The M&M's Brand Chocolate Candies Counting Book* by Barbara Barbieri McGrath uses M&M's to teach young readers to count up to ten, using the lovable M&M's characters and blue M&M's.

Storage

● **Clorox Bleach jug.** To make a carrier for game pieces, with adult supervision cut a hole in the side of an empty, clean Clorox Bleach jug opposite the handle.

● **Cool Whip tub.** Never lose dice, cards, playing pieces, and small toys again—by storing them inside a clean, empty Cool Whip canister and sealing the lid securely shut.

● **Huggies Baby Wipes box.** Store loose dice, cards, game pieces, puzzle pieces, and small toys in an empty Huggies Baby Wipes box.

● **Kleenex Tissues box.** A decorative Kleenex Tissues box, when empty, makes an excellent container for storing game pieces and playing cards.

● **Pringles can.** Use an empty Pringles can decorated with Con-Tact paper to store game pieces.

● **Scotch Packaging Tape.** Fortify the corners of game and puzzle boxes with Scotch Packaging Tape.

● **Ziploc Storage Bags.** Store game pieces in a Ziploc Storage Bag so they don't get lost.

STRANGE FACTS

● Almost every ancient culture independently developed the game of marbles.

● As early as the seventeenth century, British children played a game in which a lit candle was placed in the middle of a room and the players tried to jump over it without extinguishing the flame. The game inspired the nursery rhyme, "Jack be nimble, Jack be quick, Jack jumped over the candlestick."

● Since 1912, Cracker Jack has given out more than twenty-three billion toys.

● In 1931, Alfred Mosher Butts, a New England architect who lost his job during the Depression, entertained himself at home by trying to figure out how to turn the popular crossword puzzle into a viable board game. He originally named it "Lexiko," but eventually changed the name to "Criss-Cross Words." Over the next ten years, Butts played the game with his family and friends, fine-tuning the rules and each letter's point value. In 1948, one of his friends, James Brunot of Newton, Connecticut, persuaded Butts that the game had vast commercial potential. Brunot refined the game, copyrighted it as Scrabble, and brought it to game manufacturers.

● The word in the English language that scores the highest number of points in the game of Scrabble is *quartzy*, which scores 164 points if played across a red triple-word square with the Z on a light blue double-letter square. The word *quartzy* scores 162 points if played across two pink double-word squares with the letters *Q* and *Y* on those squares. The word scores an extra fifty points for using all seven letters in one turn.

● In the game Monopoly, the most money you can lose in one turn—playing under normal game rules—is $5,070. The most money you could conceivably lose in one trip around the board—going to jail only once—is $26,040. The game, however, comes with only $15,410.

● Monopoly is the best-selling board game in the world, sold in eighty countries and produced in twenty-six languages.

● In his play *Antony and Cleopatra*, William Shakespeare mentions billiards, though the play takes place in ancient Egypt centuries before the game was invented.

● On November 17, 1968, when the New York Jets were beating the Oakland Raiders by three points with less than a minute left in the game, NBC-TV switched from its coverage of the game to its scheduled broadcast of the movie *Heidi*. In the final fifty seconds, the Raiders scored two touchdowns, winning the game, 43–32.

● Ed McMahon began his career as an announcer at age fifteen as a "caller" at a bingo game in Maine and spent the next three years touring the state fair and carnival circuit.

Glues and Pastes

Colorful Glue

● **SueBee Honey bottle, Elmer's Glue-All,** and **McCormick Food Coloring.** Fill an empty SueBee Honey bear with Elmer's Glue-All and tint with a few drops of McCormick Food Coloring to make colorful glues.

Cornstarch Paste

● **Kingsford's Corn Starch** and **C&H Sugar.** Mix one-half cup Kingsford's Corn Starch, two tablespoons C&H Sugar, and one cup water in a pot, blending well until you achieve the consistency of paste. With adult supervision, cook the mixture over low heat until you achieve the consistency of pudding. Store in an airtight container or a Ziploc Storage Bag in the refrigerator.

Flour Paste

● **Gold Medal Flour.** Mix Gold Medal Flour and water to a pancake-batter consistency for use on paper, lightweight fabric, and cardboard.

Glue Dispenser

● **SueBee Honey bottle.** Fill a clean, empty SueBee Honey bear with Elmer's Glue-All, or any of the glues here.

Jell-O Glue and Stickers

● **Jell-O, Rubbermaid, C&H Sugar,** and **Q-Tips Cotton Swabs.** Empty one packet (1/4 ounce) Jell-O (any flavor) into a heatproof Rubbermaid container. With adult supervision, add one-quarter cup boiling water and stir with a spoon or whisk until the gelatin powder is dissolved. Add one tablespoon C&H Sugar and stir until dissolved. To make your own stickers, use a Q-Tips Cotton Swab or a small paint brush to spread a thin coat of the gum on the back of a piece of paper, cut-out shapes, or a photograph, and let dry. To use, simply moisten the gum with your tongue or a damp sponge and adhere. Store the Jell-O glue in the refrigerator. To use the hardened gelatin, set the container in a pan of hot water to turn the gelatin back into liquid form.

Milk Glue

● **Carnation NonFat Dry Milk, Heinz White Vinegar,** and **Arm & Hammer Baking Soda.** You can make glue from milk by simply adding one-third cup vinegar to one cup Carnation NonFat Dry Milk in a wide-mouthed jar. When the milk separates into curds and whey, pour off the liquid and wash it away. (Cheese is made from curds. White glue is made from a protein in the curds called casein.) Add one-quarter cup water and one tablespoon Arm & Hammer Baking Soda. When the bubbling stops, you've got glue.

Paper Paste

● **Gold Medal Flour** and **C&H Sugar.** Mix one-quarter cup Gold Medal Flour, one-quarter cup C&H Sugar, and one cup water in a saucepan. With adult supervision, simmer over low heat, stirring constantly until the mixture achieves the consistency of pudding. Let cool. Spread the paste with a paintbrush or a wooden tongue depressor. Store in an airtight container or Ziploc Storage Bag in the refrigerator.

Rice Glue

● **Uncle Ben's Converted Brand Rice.** Mix one-half cup Uncle Ben's Converted Brand Rice with one-half cup water and after stirring for a while, you get glue.

● **Cutex Nail Polish Remover.** If you ever glue your fingers together with Krazy Glue, use Cutex Nail Polish Remover as a solvent to dissolve the glue. Then wash clean with soap and water.

● **Miracle Whip.** Miracle Whip works miracles when it comes to removing glue from skin or tabletops. Simply put some Miracle Whip on the tip of your finger and rub it over the glue, which will slowly dissolve.

● **Jif Peanut Butter.** A dab of Jif Peanut Butter removes the sticky residue left by Band-Aids, the sticky labels or price tags on glass items, and glue from any surface.

● **Pam Cooking Spray.** Give dried glue on skin or any surface a quick spritz of Pam Cooking Spray, and then wipe clean. The oils in the cooking spray dissolve the adhesive in the glue.

● **Purell Instant Hand Sanitizer.** Purell, the soapless, antibacterial hand sanitizer, removes adhesive from skin, walls, and tabletops.

● **WD-40.** Clean dried glue from any hard surface with WD-40. Simply spray with WD-40, let sit thirty seconds, and wipe clean with soapy water.

● **Wesson Corn Oil.** Clean glue off skin or any surface with a drop of Wesson Corn Oil, and then wipe clean.

Sugar Paste

● **C&H Sugar, Gold Medal Flour,** and **McCormick Alum.** In a saucepan, mix together one-quarter cup C&H Sugar, one-quarter cup Gold Medal Flour, and one-half teaspoon McCormick Alum. Slowly add one cup water, stirring well. With adult supervision, boil until clear and smooth, stirring the mixture constantly. Add three-quarters cup water, blending well. Let cool. Spread with a paintbrush or tongue depressor. Store in an airtight container in the refrigerator.

Tools

● **Forster Toothpicks.** Dip one end of a Forster Toothpick into glue to apply small drops.

● **Q-Tips Cotton Swabs.** A Q-Tips Cotton Swab doubles as an excellent brush for dabbing on glue for crafts projects.

STRANGE FACTS

● Before the invention of self-sealing envelopes, people used hot wax to seal envelopes shut.

● In 1804, French chemist Armand Seguin erroneously concluded that the ingredient in the bark of the cinchona tree that cured malaria was gelatin. Seguin published his wrong findings, prompting physicians to treat their malaria patients with clarified glue.

● In 1929, the Borden Company purchased the Casein Company of America, the leading manufacturer of glues made from casein, a milk protein. Borden introduced its first nonfood consumer product, Casco Glue, in 1932.

● While promoted by a spokesbull and made by a milk company, Elmer's Glue-All is a synthetic resin glue that does not contain casein.

● Cyanoacrylate (an adhesive substance sold as Krazy Glue or Super Glue) was invented by accident. In 1942, Dr. Harry Coover of Kodak Laboratories concocted cyanoacrylate glue while trying to make optically clear plastic for gun sights. Nine years later, while seeking a heat-resistant acrylate polymer for jet canopies with Coover, Dr. Fred Joyner (who also worked at Kodak Laboratories) spread a film of ethyl cyanoacrylate between two refractometer prisms and discovered that the prisms were glued together. Coover suddenly realized the potential uses for the adhesive, and Kodak marketed the glue in 1958 as Eastman Compound #910.

● The glue on Israeli postage stamps is certified kosher.

Greeting Cards and Wrapping Paper

Decoupage Greeting Cards

● **Elmer's Glue-All** and **Dixie Cups.** Cut out pictures from a glossy magazine or catalog (or cut out shapes from colored construction paper or decorative wrapping paper). Pour some Elmer's Glue-All into a Dixie Cup and using a paint brush, paint the glue on a piece of cardboard and place the cut-out pictures on the glued surface. Let dry. Paint a coat of glue over the finished piece of cardboard. Glue the finished piece of artwork to the front of a folded piece of construction paper to make a greeting card. For more ways to make decoupage, see page 36.

Designer Envelopes

● **Elmer's Glue-All** and **Avery Mailing Labels.** Carefully take apart an envelope and flatten it out to use as a pattern. Tear out a colorful page from a magazine or catalog and place the envelope pattern over the page. Using a pen or pencil, trace around the envelope pattern and cut out the resulting shape. Fold the resulting shape into an envelope and glue the seams into place with Elmer's Glue-All. Adhere two Avery Address Labels to the front of the envelope for the address and return address. (After inserting a letter, you can seal the envelope with Elmer's Glue-All, Scotch Tape, or any of glues on pages 70–72.)

Sealing Wax

● **Cover Girl NailSlicks Classic Red Nail Polish.** Use Cover Girl NailSlicks Classic Red Nail Polish the same way you'd use wax to seal an envelope or letter.

● **Crayola Crayons.** Have an adult light a match and then hold it under an unwrapped Crayola Crayon to drip some of the wax over the envelope's seal as sealing wax. You can use a decorative button or a coin to imprint a fancy design in the colored wax.

Sparkle Greeting Cards

● **Elmer's Glue-All** and **Reynolds Wrap.** In a bowl, mix equal parts Elmer's Glue-All and water. Crinkle up a paper-size piece of Reynolds Wrap, and then flatten it out on a table top. Tear several different pieces of colored tissue paper into strips and small pieces. (To make your own colored tissue paper, see "Wrapping Paper" below.)

Using a paint brush, paint the glue solution on the aluminum foil. Place a piece of colored tissue on the aluminum foil and paint over it with more glue solution. Add more pieces of tissue paper, painting over each additional piece with glue solution.

Placing different colored tissue papers over each other creates new colors. If you wish, you can sprinkle colored rice (see page 109), beans, pasta, or glitter over your wet painting. Let dry overnight. Wrap the finished foil around a small piece of cardboard and glue it to the front of a folded piece of construction paper to make a greeting card. Or use large sheets of paper to create wrapping paper.

Wrapping Paper

● **Aqua Net Hair Spray.** Make your own gift wrapping paper by spraying Aqua Net Hair Spray on the comic section from the Sunday paper to seal in the ink and give the paper a shiny gloss.

● **McCormick Food Coloring.** Add five drops McCormick Food

Coloring to one cup water, making one cup for each one of the four colors. Stack several sheets of white tissue paper on top of each other, fold them in half, in half again, and in half again. Dip each one of the four corners into a different color solution without soaking the paper. Let the tissue dry on newspaper, unfold, and then (with adult supervision) iron flat.

● **USA Today.** Use pages of *USA Today* to improvise gift-wrapping paper.

STRANGE FACTS

● The first commercially produced Valentine's Day cards were printed in 1803, forty years before the first commercially produced Christmas cards.

● In 1843, London artist John Calcott Horsley, commissioned by wealthy businessman Sir Henry Cole, designed the first commercially printed Christmas card. The card featured an illustration of a large family enjoying a festive Christmas party and was inscribed with the words, "A Merry Christmas and a Happy New Year to You." The card outraged members of the British Temperance Movement, who sternly criticized Horsley for depicting children drinking wine.

● In the United States, Richard Pease printed the first commercial Christmas card sometime between 1850 and 1852 to advertise Pease's Great Variety Store in Albany, New York. The card pictured Santa Claus and a black slave setting the Christmas dinner table.

● In 1875, Boston lithographer Louis Prang, a German native, became the "father of the American Christmas card" when he began printing expensive cards depicting various floral arrangements.

● In 1931, Hugh Troy, described as "America's leading practical joker," sent out Christmas cards with a faint design of meandering swirls, printed with nothing but a border and the ambiguous message, "Soak this card in tepid water five minutes." Many of his friends, unable to get a design or message to appear, figured they had used the wrong temperature water. Others saw images appear where nothing was meant to appear.

Jewelry

Baking Soda Beads
● **Arm & Hammer Baking Soda, Kingsford's Corn Starch,** and **Forster Toothpicks.** In a pot, mix two cups Arm & Hammer Baking Soda, one cup Kingford's Corn Starch, and one-and-a-half cups water until smooth. With adult supervision, boil over medium heat until the mixture thickens to the consistency of dough. Let cool. Knead into a smooth, pliable dough. Mold the dough into beads and pierce a hole in each bead with a Forster Toothpick. Let dry. Paint with bright colors. To string the beads together to make a necklace or bracelet, see "String" on page 80.

Bread Beads
● **Wonder Bread, Elmer's Glue-All,** and **Forster Toothpicks.** Remove the crust from three slices of Wonder Bread. Mash the bread in a bowl and add three teaspoons Elmer's Glue-All. Knead until the dough is no longer sticky. Roll the dough into little balls, and then pierce each with a Forster Toothpick. Let dry for twelve hours, paint the beads in bright colors, and let dry. To string the beads together, see "String" on page 80.

Dough Beads
● **Gold Medal Flour, Morton Salt, Wesson Vegetable Oil,** and **Forster Toothpicks.** Using a fork, mix two cups Gold Medal Flour, one cup Morton Salt, one tablespoon Wesson Vegetable Oil, and one cup hot water in a large bowl. When the dough thickens, knead it with your hands until the dough is firm. If the dough is too sticky, add more flour. If the dough is too stiff, add more water. Knead the dough on a cutting board for roughly ten minutes, until the dough becomes smooth. Roll out the dough into small balls to make beads of

various shapes and sizes (circles, squares, triangles, fruit shapes, etc.) and pierce each bead with a Forster Toothpick. Let dry naturally, or with adult supervision set your oven to 200 degrees Fahrenheit, place the beads on a baking tray, and bake until completely dry (between five and eight hours). Paint the beads bright colors and let dry. To string the beads together, see "String" on page 80.

Foil Beads

● **Reynolds Wrap** and **Forster Toothpicks.** With adult supervision, use a pair of scissors to carefully cut Reynolds Wrap into four-inch squares. Poke a Forster Toothpick through the center of a square and scrunch up the aluminum foil to form a small ball around the toothpick. Remove the toothpick, leaving an aluminum foil bead with a hole through it. Repeat until you have made as many beads as you wish. To string the beads together to make a necklace or bracelet, see "String" on page 80.

Froot Loops Necklace

● **Oral-B Dental Floss** and **Kellogg's Froot Loops.** Cut a piece of Oral-B Dental Floss long enough to make a necklace, and tied one end to a piece of Froot Loops cereal as a stopper bead. Thread the free end of the dental floss through pieces of Froot Loop cereals, using any pattern you like, to create a necklace. When you're done, cut off the stopper bead and tie the two free ends together.

Jewelry Box

● **Elmer's Glue-All** and **Huggies Baby Wipes box.** With adult supervision, using scissors, cut shapes from felt or colored construction paper and glue them with Elmer's Glue-All to a clean, empty Huggies Baby Wipes box to create a jewelry box.

Macaroni Jewelry

● **McCormick Food Coloring, Kraft Macaroni & Cheese,** and **Reynolds Cut-Rite Wax Paper.** Add a few drops of McCormick Food Coloring to a bowl of water. Dip dry macaroni noodles into the water and drain. Place the colored noodles on a sheet of Reynolds Cut-Rite Wax Paper and let dry. To string the macaroni together to make a necklace, see "String" on page 80.

Pressed-Paper Pulp Beads

● **Kleenex Tissues, Gold Medal Flour, Reynolds Cut-Rite Wax Paper,** and **Forster Toothpicks.** Tear several Kleenex Tissues into small pieces, place in a bowl, and cover with warm water. Let the tissues soak for several hours until they soften into mush, and then mash with a spoon. Strain the mixture through a sieve, lightly squeezing out the water, but leaving the pulp damp. Place the pulp back in the bowl and mix with one tablespoon Gold Medal Flour. Strain out the excess water, again leaving the pulp damp like clay. Mold the pulp into bead shapes, place the beads on a sheet of Reynolds Cut-Rite Wax Paper, and let dry in a warm spot. When the beads are nearly dry, pierce a hole through each bead with a Forster Toothpick. Let dry completely. Paint the beads in bright colors. Let dry. To string the beads together to make a necklace or bracelet, see "String" on page 80.

Rolled Paper Beads

● **Forster Toothpicks** and **Elmer's Glue-All.** Tear full-page, color photos from a glossy magazine or catalog. Using a ruler and a pencil, mark out a series of elongated triangles on the back of the magazine page, measuring 1/2-inch wide by the length of the page. (For wider beads, make the triangles one inch wide. With adult supervision, use a pair of scissors to cut out the triangles. Starting at the wide end of each triangle, roll the paper around a Forster Toothpick and secure the end in place with a dab of Elmer's Glue-All.

Hold for a moment to let the glue dry, and then slide the bead off the toothpick. To string the beads together to make a necklace or bracelet, see "String" below.

Straw Necklaces
● **Glad Drinking Straws.** With adult supervision, use a pair of scissors to cut up colorful Glad Drinking Straws and run a piece of yarn through them to make necklaces and bracelets. (See "String" below.)

String
● **Oral-B Dental Floss** and **Elmer's Glue-All.** Cut a piece of Oral-B Dental Floss the length you desire for a necklace or bracelet, tie one end loosely, but securely, to one bead (to prevent the other beads from falling off the string, and then thread the other end of the floss through the beads. The sturdiness of the waxed floss enables you to thread the beads without using a needle. After threading all the beads, remove the stopper bead, and tie the two ends together. (Applying a dab of Elmer's Glue-All on all knots will help secure them in place.)

STRANGE FACTS
● In 1667, the *Waken Van Amsterdam,* a Dutch ship carrying forty crates of gold and four tons of uncut diamonds, sank. In 1983, the government of Iceland located a sunken wooden ship and spent millions of dollars to raise the *Waken Van Amsterdam*—only to bring up a German trawler that had sunk in 1903 carrying a cargo of herring.
● According to the U.S. Census Bureau, as of 2002 the United States was home to 28,914 jewelry stores.
● Jerry Lewis's eldest son, Gary Lewis, and his rock group, The Playboys, recorded the hit song "This Diamond Ring."
● The diamond, made from pure carbon and one of the hardest substances known, turns from a solid directly into a gas at 3500 degrees Celsius, a process known as sublimation.
● Richard Burton gave Elizabeth Taylor some of the world's most magnificent jewelry, including the Rupp Diamond and the Lap Regina Pearl.

Miscellaneous Fun

Bird Seed Art

● **Elmer's Glue-All** and **Hartz Parakeet Seed.** Paint a design in Elmer's Glue-All on construction paper, and then cover the glue with Hartz Parakeet Seed and let dry.

Book Covers

● **Con-Tact Paper.** Use clear Con-Tact Paper to cover and protect school books.

● **Con-Tact Paper.** Hide the title of a paperback book by giving the book a mystery cover made from colored Con-Tact Paper.

Eraser

● **Wonder Bread.** To erase pencil marks from paper, simply peel off the crust from a slice of Wonder Bread and rub the white part of the bread over the pencil marks.

Goldfish Aquarium

● **Dixie Paper Plates, Crayola Crayons, Elmer's Glue-All, Pepperidge Farm Goldfish, Scotch Tape,** and **Saran Wrap.** Color the inside of a Dixie Paper Plate with blue Crayola Crayons to create an underwater seascape. Using Elmer's Glue-All, glue Pepperidge Farm Goldfish to the inside of the plate to look like the fish are swimming. Cut large circular hole in the center of a second paper plate to create a porthole. With Scotch Tape, tape the two plates together so they are face to face. Tape a sheet of Saran Wrap over the hole to create the illusion of the glass pane of a fish tank.

Leaf Art
● **Reynolds Cut-Rite Wax Paper** and **Crayola Crayons.**
Place an autumn leaf or several autumn leaves between two sheets of Reynolds Cut-Rite Wax Paper, and then place the wax paper between two sheets of brown paper. With adult supervision, press with a warm iron to seal, and then trim the paper around the leaves. To create a more abstract effect, add crayon shavings between the wax paper sheets before ironing. The iron will melt the wax, adding swirling colors.

Leaf Placemat
● **Con-Tact Paper.** Peel off the adhesive backing from a sheet of clear Con-Tact Paper the size of a placemat and lay it sticky-side up on a tabletop. Place leaves on the adhesive paper. Peal the adhesive backing from a second sheet of clear Con-Tract paper, the same size as the first, and lay it sticky side down to the first sheet, covering the leaves. Smooth out the sheets, starting from the center and working your way out to the edges to remove any air bubbles. With adult supervision, use a pair of scissors to trim the sides of the placemat.

Memo Board
● **Con-Tact Paper** and **Velcro.** Create an instant memo board by covering a sheet of cardboard with clear Con-Tact Paper, adhering to a wall or refrigerator door with Velcro, and writing on it with an erasable marker.

Newspaper Clippings
● **Phillips' Milk of Magnesia, Canada Dry Club Soda,** and **Bounty Paper Towels.** To preserve a newspaper clipping, dissolve one capful of Phillips' Milk of Magnesia in one quart Canada Dry Club Soda. Let set in refrigerator eight hours. Shake well and

pour into a shallow pan or tray to accommodate the flat newspaper clipping. Soak the clipping for one hour, and then blot between two sheets of Bounty Paper Towels and place on a screen to dry. This prevents yellowing by neutralizing the acid in the paper.

Pencil Holders

● **Campbell's Soup.** A clean, empty Campbell's Soup can doubles as an effective pencil holder. Decorate the can by wrapping it with a piece of colored construction paper festooned with paint, crayon, glitter, or colored macaroni (see page 109). Or spray a clean, empty Campbell's Soup can with a coat of spray paint. With adult supervision, glue several painted cans together with a glue gun to make a desk organizer for pencils and pens.

● **Con-Tact Paper.** Make a pencil holder by wrapping a clean, empty tin can with your favorite Con-Tact Paper.

● **Crisco All-Vegetable Shortening.** A clean, empty Crisco All-Vegetable Shortening can makes an excellent container for holding pens and pencils. Decorate the can by wrapping it with a piece of colored construction paper festooned with paint, crayon, glitter, or colored macaroni (see page 109).

● **Elmer's Glue-All, Dixie Cups,** and **Maxwell House Coffee.** With adult supervision, use a pair of scissors to cut out words, pictures, or artwork from glossy magazine or catalogs. Mix equal parts Elmer's Glue-All and water in a Dixie Cup. With a paintbrush, paint the glue on a clean, empty Maxwell House Coffee can and adhere the pictures to the can. Cover the pictures with a coat of the glue solution to hold down the edges and laminate the pictures.

● **Maxwell House Coffee.** Nothing works better as pencil holder than a clean, empty Maxwell House Coffee can. Decorate the can by wrapping it with a piece of colored construction paper festooned with paint, crayon, glitter, or colored macaroni (see page 109).

Placemats

● **Con-Tact Paper.** To make placemats from children's artwork, cover both sides of a child's drawing, painting, or construction paper collage with clear Con-Tact Paper and cut to size.

Scratch and Sniff Art Work

● **Jell-O.** To make scratch and sniff artwork, mix the contents of one packet of Jell-O with just enough water to make a thick paste. Let kids finger paint with it on poster board, let dry, and then scratch and sniff.

Shoes

● **Con-Tact Paper.** To teach a toddler which shoe goes on which foot, trace the toddler's feet onto brightly colored Con-Tact Paper, cut out the foot prints, and adhere them to a sturdy board. The child can then match the shoe with the correct foot print.

Storage

● **Cool Whip tub.** Organize ribbons, beads, glues, and strings in empty Cool Whip canisters.

● **Huggies Baby Wipes box.** Organize ribbons, beads, glues, and strings in empty Huggies Baby Wipes boxes.

● **Pringles can** and **Con-Tact Paper.** Use an empty Pringles can decorated with Con-Tact paper to store paintbrushes, colored pencils, and crayons.

● **Ziploc Storage Bags.** Buttons, beads, and various odds and ends store well in Ziploc Storage Bags.

Videotape and DVD Boxes

● **Con-Tact Paper.** Decorate home video boxes or DVD boxes with unique labels made from Con-Tact Paper, making them easier to organize and find.

STRANGE FACTS

● Pop artist Andy Warhol achieved world reknown for his enormous paintings of Campbell's Soup Cans.

● Every April Fool's Day in Eugene, Oregon, the Maude Kerns Art Center holds the Jell-O Art Show, better known as "Jell-O-Rama," featuring works of local artists using Jell-O as a medium.

● In 1996, artist Michael Gonzalez's show at the Huntington Beach Art Center featured paintings incorporating Wonder Bread wrappers.

Musical Instruments

Drums
● **Maxwell House Coffee can** and **Con-Tact Paper.** Decorate the outside of a clean, empty Maxwell House Coffee can with Con-Tact Paper (or paint, construction paper, or decoupage), and seal the plastic lid in place. For drumsticks, you can use unsharpened pencils (hitting the plastic lid or the metal bottom with the eraser tips). To achieve a better drum sound, use a can opener to remove the metal bottom of the coffee can and cover the opening with a second plastic lid.

● **Quaker Oats, Con-Tact Paper,** and **Bounty Paper Towels.** Glue the lid on an empty Quaker Oats canister and decorate the cardboard container by covering it with Con-Tact Paper (or decorate with paint, or a picture on a piece of construction paper that is glued in place). Use the cardboard tube from an empty roll of Bounty Paper Towels as a drumstick.

Kleenex Box Guitar
● **Kleenex Tissues, Bounty Paper Towels,** and **Scotch Tape.** Peel off the plastic from the slot of a rectangular box of Kleenex Tissues. Against one of the short sides of the box, place the end of a cardboard tube from an empty roll of Bounty Paper Towels and trace around it with a pen or pencil to make a circle. With adult supervision, use a pair of scissors to cut out the circle. Insert the cardboard

tube into the hole for two inches, and secure in place with Scotch Tape. Wrap three or four rubber bands around the box lengthwise so that they pass over the oval hole. Decorate the guitar any way you wish. To play the guitar, simply strum the rubber bands.

Maracas

- **Orville Redenbacher's Gourmet Popping Corn, Quaker Oats,** and **Scotch Packaging Tape.** To make a maraca, put a handful of unpopped Orville Redenbacher's Gourmet Popping Corn inside a clean, empty Quaker Oats canister and seal the cardboard container shut with Scotch Packaging Tape. Decorate the canister with paint, glitter, and shapes cut from construction paper.
- **Uncle Ben's Converted Brand Rice.** If you don't have any Orville Redenbacher's Gourmet Popping Corn, substitute a handful of Uncle Ben's Converted Brand Rice in your homemade maracas.

Megaphone

- **Clorox Bleach jug.** Make a powerful megaphone by removing the cap and, with adult supervision, cutting off the bottom of an empty, clean Clorox Bleach bottle. Decorate the outside of the jug as you wish.
- **Gatorade bottle.** Remove the cap and, with adult supervision, cut off the bottom of an empty, clean Gatorade bottle to make a clear megaphone.

Rainmaker

- **Reynolds Cut-Rite Wax Paper, Bounty Paper Towels, Scotch Tape,** and **Uncle Ben's Converted Brand Rice.** With adult supervision, use a pair of scissors to cut two circular pieces of Reynolds Cut-Rite Wax Paper to fit over the opposite ends of the cardboard tube from an empty roll of Bounty Paper Towels. With Scotch Tape, secure one circle of wax paper over one end of the tube. Pour a small handful of Uncle Ben's Converted Brand Rice into the open end of the cardboard tube. With Scotch Tape, secure the second circle of wax paper over the remaining open end of the tube. To use the rainmaker, simply hold the tube in a vertical position and slowly turn it upside down, allowing the rice to tumble gently inside the tube to the other end.

Slinky Music
● **Slinky.** Tie a twelve-inch piece of string to each end of a metal Slinky, and then hold the end of each string over your ears. Let the Slinky droop down in a big arc and move your head up and down. You'll hear the weird sounds generated by the flexing coil.

Straw Horn
● **Glad Drinking Straws.** Chew on the end of plastic Glad Drinking Straw to flatten one inch of the end. With adult supervision, use a pair of scissors to carefully trim the flattened end to a 'V,' like a pencil point. Put the flattened, pointed end of the straw in your mouth, just behind your lips, and blow hard. Experiment by cutting small pieces off the end of the straw. The shorter you cut the straw, the higher the pitch of the sound.

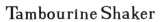

Tambourine Shaker
● **Dixie Paper Plates, Crayola Crayons, Kellogg's Froot Loops,** and **Scotch Tape.** Decorate the outside bottom of two Dixie Paper Plates using Crayola Crayons. Place a handful of Kellogg's Froot Loops in the center of one place, place the other plate face down on top of it, and staple the edges together. Cover the edges of the plate with Scotch Tape.

STRANGE FACTS
● At the 1980 Kuhmo Music Festival, Soviet cellist Agustinas Vassiliauskas rose to the podium for a third time to bow to the

audience for their standing ovation. He tripped, fell, and smashed his 300-year-old Ruggieri cello.

● The English horn is neither English nor a horn. The wind instrument is actually an alto oboe (a double-reed pipe like the oboe and bassoon) developed in 1760 by Italian composer Giuseppe Ferlendis of Bergamo.

● Nero did not fiddle while Rome burned. The violin was not developed in Italy until 1500 years after Nero's death. Nero may have played the lyre, but definitely not the violin.

● Rock musician Sting got his nickname for wearing a yellow-and-black striped shirt until it literally fell apart. His real name is Gordon Sumner.

● Albert Von Tilzer, who composed the music to the song "Take Me Out to the Ball Game" in 1908, did not see a baseball game until more than twenty years after the song's release.

● While trying to break into acting, Jack Lemmon played piano in a New York City beer hall.

● John Lennon's Aunt Mimi, who raised the future Beatle in her suburban home, relegated her nephew's guitar playing to the porch.

Paints

Black-Light Paint
● **Era.** Use liquid Era to paint designs on a white poster board, let dry (turning invisible), and then turn on a black light in a dark room to see the phosphorescent art.

● **Liquid Tide.** With a paintbrush, paint designs or a message on a white poster board. Let sit until the liquid detergent dries, turning invisible. In a dark room, turn on a black light and hold the poster near the light. The liquid detergent painted on the white poster board appears invisible in ordinary light, but glows purplish-white under the black light.

● **Murine Tears.** Write or draw on skin or paper with Murine eye drops, let dry, and then illuminate under black light in a dark room. The drawing or writing glows under black light as fluorescent yellow.

Crinkle Paintings
● **Bubble Wrap.** Using a paintbrush, give a piece of white paper a thick coat of water. Using watercolors, work quickly to paint big pools of bright colors on the wet paper, allowing the colors to flow out and blend with each other. Place a sheet of Bubble Wrap, bubble-side down, on top of the wet painting, patting down gently. Let sit overnight to dry, and then peel off the Bubble Wrap, revealing unique patterns and textures on your painting.

● **Reynolds Cut-Rite Wax Paper.** Instead of using Bubble Wrap (as explained on page 89), crumple up a sheet of Reynolds Cut-Rite Wax Paper (roughly twice the size of the sheet of paper used), place it on top of the wet painting, and pat down gently.

● **Reynolds Wrap.** Rather than using Bubble Wrap (as explained on page 89), crumple up a sheet of Reynolds Wrap (roughly twice the size of the sheet of paper used), place it on top of the wet painting, and pat down gently.

● **Saran Wrap.** Rather than using Bubble Wrap (as explained above), crumple up a sheet of Saran Wrap (roughly twice the size of the sheet of paper used), place it on top of the wet painting, and pat down gently.

Dough Paint

● **Gold Medal Flour, Morton Salt, McCormick Food Coloring,** and **Ziploc Storage Bags** (or **Dawn Dishwashing Liquid bottle** or **Heinz Ketchup bottle**). Mix one-quarter cup Gold Medal Flour, one-quarter cup Morton Salt, and one-quarter cup water in a large bowl. Mix in several drops of McCormick Food Coloring; use as many as you wish to achieve whatever color you desire. Pour the solution into a Ziploc Storage Bag, seal the bag, and snip off a bottom corner with a pair of scissors. (Or, if you prefer, pour the mixture into plastic squeeze bottle such as a clean, used Dawn Dishwashing Liquid bottle or a Heinz Ketchup Bottle.) Squeeze the plastic bag to paint a design onto cardboard or poster board or to paint a papier-mâché sculpture.

Egg Tempera Paint

● **Crayola Chalk** and **Dixie Cups.** Using a mortar and pestle, grind up a piece of colored Crayola Chalk. In a Dixie Cup, mix one egg yolk with a little water to create the consistency of paint. Add a few pinches of the colored chalk powder and stir until you create the color you desire. Repeat in different Dixie Cups with different colored chalk to create different colors. Paint on heavy paper.

● **Kool-Aid** and **Dixie Cups.** In a Dixie Cup, mix one egg yolk with a little water to create the consistency of paint. Add a few pinches of any color Kool-Aid powdered mix and stir until you create the color you desire. Repeat with different colored Kool-Aid in different Dixie Cups to create different colors. Paint on heavy paper.

● **Tang** and **Dixie Cups**. In a Dixie Cup, mix one egg yolk with a little water to create the consistency of paint. Add a few pinches of Tang powdered mix and stir until you create the color you desire. Paint on heavy paper.

Glue Painting
● **Elmer's Glue-All** and **Kiwi Shoe Polish.** Using a pencil, draw a simple design on a piece of cardboard. By squeezing glue from a bottle of Elmer's Glue-All, draw over the lines of your design on the cardboard. If you desire, add additional squiggles and dots of glue in and around your design. Let dry overnight. Paint over the dried glue and cardboard with gold acrylic paint. Let dry. To achieve an antique look, dampen a soft cloth with black Kiwi Shoe Polish and rub the color all over the painting, and then wipe off the excess shoe polish. You can also use this technique to make a picture frame.

Grape Juice Paint
● **Welch's 100% Purple Grape Juice.** For a terrific substitute for purple paint, use Welch's 100% Purple Grape Juice on a sheet of white paper. (Be careful not to stain furniture, clothes, or carpeting with grape juice.)

Jell-O Paint
● **Jell-O** and **Dixie Cups.** Place one tablespoon Jell-O powder in a Dixie Cup. Use different cups for different colors. With adult supervision, add three tablespoons boiling water to each cup, stirring to dissolve the powder completely. Let cool, and then within thirty minutes (before the gelatin sets) use a paintbrush to paint the colors on a sheet of paper. Let dry for several hours. (Paintings may be a little sticky when dry.)

Ketchup and Mustard Paint
● **French's Mustard** and **Heinz Ketchup.** For an excellent

substitute for yellow paint, use a paintbrush to paint French's mustard on a white sheet of paper. Heinz Ketchup makes excellent red paint.

Milk Paint

● **Carnation Nonfat Dry Milk** and **McCormick Food Coloring.** Mix 1-1/2 cups Carnation Nonfat Dry Milk and one-half cup water until it is the consistency of paint. Blend in McCormick Food Coloring to make the desired hue. Thin the paint by adding more water; thicken the paint by adding more powdered milk. Brush on as you would any other paint. Let the first coat dry for at least 24 hours before adding a second coat. Let the second dry for three days.

● **Carnation Nonfat Dry Milk** and **Kool-Aid.** Instead of using food coloring in the recipe above, use a packet of Kool-Aid drink mix.

● **Carnation Nonfat Dry Milk** and **Tang.** Rather than using food coloring in the first recipe above, use a few teaspoons of Tang powdered drink mix to make orange paint.

Paintbrushes

● **Forster Clothes Pins** and **Scotch-Brite Heavy Duty Scrub Sponge.** To improvise a paintbrush, clip a Forster clothes pin to a small square of sponge or foam rubber.

● **Q-Tips Cotton Swabs.** Use a Q-Tips Cotton Swab as a paint brush.

Pointillism

● **Crayola Chalk, Q-Tips Cotton Swabs,** and **Forster Toothpicks.** To create a painting using only dots (a technique called pointillism), use a piece of yellow Crayola Chalk to lightly sketch your drawing on a sheet of white paper. Then use a Q-Tips Cotton

Swab dipped in paint to create dots of paint over your drawing. Use a different Q-Tips Cotton Swab for each color. To create smaller dots, use Forster Toothpicks dipped in paint.

Pudding Paint
● **Gold Medal Flour, C&H Sugar, Morton Salt, McCormick Food Coloring,** and **Dixie Cups.** Mix two cups Gold Medal Flour, one-half cup C&H Sugar, three tablespoons Morton Salt, and five cups water in a saucepan and, with adult supervision, warm over medium heat until the mixture becomes thick and starts to bubble. Let cool. In four separate Dixie Cups, mix the pudding with a different color food coloring, making blue, red, green, and yellow pudding paint. Paint on cardboard or poster board using a paintbrush or Popsicle stick.

Salt Paint
● **Morton Salt.** Mix enough salt into liquid tempera paint to create a thick, gritty paint. When painted on paper, the salt paint creates a sandy texture when it dries.

Snow Painting
● **McCormick Food Coloring.** On a snow day, put a teaspoon of food coloring in a spray bottle filled with water and spray designs on snow.

Sparkle Painting
● **Elmer's Glue-All** and **Reynolds Wrap.** In a bowl, mix equal parts Elmer's Glue-All and water. Crinkle up a paper-size piece of Reynolds Wrap, and then flatten it out on a table top. Tear several different pieces of colored tissue paper into strips and small pieces. (To make your own colored tissue paper, see page 75). Using a paintbrush, paint the glue solution on the aluminum foil. Place a piece of colored tissue on the aluminum foil and paint over it with more glue solution. Add more pieces of tissue paper, painting over each additional piece with glue solution. Placing different colored tissue paper over each other creates new colors. If you wish you can sprinkle colored rice

(see page 109), beans, pasta, or glitter over your wet painting. Let dry overnight. You can wrap the finished foil around a piece of cardboard (which can be hung up on the wall); glue it to a folded piece of construction paper to make a greeting card; wrap it around a clean, empty can to make a pencil holder or flower pot; or use it as gift wrapping paper.

Spatter Painting

● **Oral-B Toothbrushes.** Place a piece of paper inside a small cardboard box and place leaves, stencils, or flowers on the paper. Cover the opening of the box with a sheet of metal screening secured in place with rubber bands. Dip an Oral-B Toothbrush in paint and scrub it over the screen, allowing the paint to spatter over the paper. Remove the screen and various objects and let the painting dry.

Sponge Painting

● **Scotch-Brite Heavy Duty Scrub Sponge.** Carefully tear a thin strip of sponge off the edges of the sponge to avoid making straight lines when you paint. Dip the sponge in paint, dab it onto scrap paper until you like the intensity of the pattern, and then dab a sheet of paper. Use different sponges with different colors to achieve the design you desire. With adult supervision, you can also use a pair of scissors to cut the sponge into different shapes (such as squares, circles, triangles, or stars).

Stain

● **Kiwi Shoe Polish.** Use Kiwi Shoe Polish to stain wood to a high polish. Repeat to achieve a deeper color. It's inexpensive, easy to apply, and leaves a high gloss finish.

Storage

● **Cool Whip tub.** Use empty Cool Whip canisters to mix and store paints.

● **Crisco All-Vegetable Shortening can.** A clean, empty Crisco All-Vegetable Shortening can makes an excellent container for mixing and storing paints.

● **Arm & Hammer Baking Soda.** Just sprinkle Arm & Hammer Baking Soda over spilled paint or ink and wipe with a damp cloth or paper towel.

● **Dawn Dishwashing Liquid.** To make poster paints easy to remove from clothes, mix a few drops of Dawn Dishwashing Liquid into poster paint and mix well. This way, if you get the paint on your clothes, it will wash out easily.

● **Downy Fabric Softener.** To keep paintbrushes soft and smooth, add a drop of Downy Fabric Softener to the final rinse when cleaning paint from the bristles.

● **Gillette Foamy Shaving Cream.** To clean paint, glue, pencil marks, and ink from a tabletop, rub Gillette Foamy Shaving Cream over the surface, and then wipe clean with a damp sponge.

● **Huggies Baby Wipes.** To clean paint or ink from skin or surfaces, simply wipe clean with Huggies Baby Wipes.

● **Lubriderm.** Lubriderm Moisturizing Lotion removes oil-based paint and stain from hands more gently than turpentine.

● **Murphy Oil Soap.** Murphy Oil Soap removes permanent marker from desks and tabletops.

● **Pond's Cold Cream.** To remove permanent marker from skin, just smear a dab of Pond's Cold Cream over the ink and wipe clean.

● **Purell.** Use Purell hand sanitizer to remove paint and ink from skin.

● **Gerber Baby Food jars.** Clean, empty Gerber Baby Food jars make excellent containers to store paints.

Straw Painting

● **Glad Drinking Straws.** Place a small puddle of paint on a piece of paper, and then blow through a Glad Drinking Straw to send lines of the paint in different directions. Let dry.

Tennis Ball Rolling
● **Wilson Tennis Balls** and **Scotch Tape.** Tape the corners of a large piece of paper to the bottom of a large box. Fill each of several bowls with a different colored tempera paint. Place a Wilson Tennis Ball in each bowl of paint, and then place the tennis balls on the paper taped inside the box. Tip the box so the tennis balls roll around on the paper. Repeat until you're satisfied with the results. You can use Scotch Tape to temporarily tape smaller pieces of paper or stencil designs over the large piece of paper before rolling the paint-covered balls. When you're done, lift off the smaller pieces of paper, leaving behind unpainted shapes.

Watercolors
● **Arm & Hammer Baking Soda, Gold Medal Flour, C&H Sugar,** and **Kool-Aid.** Mix two tablespoons Arm & Hammer Baking Soda, two tablespoons Gold Medal Flour, two teaspoons C&H Sugar, and the contents of one packet of Kool-Aid of your choice. Add two tablespoons water and stir until the fizzing ceases. Use immediately as paint or pour the paints into a plastic ice cube tray and let harden for future use, adding a few drops of water when you're ready to paint.
● **Dixie Cups** and **Kool-Aid.** Pour one teaspoon water into a Dixie Cup and add a few pinches of any flavor Kool-Aid. Repeat in several Dixie Cups to make as many watercolors as you desire. Simply use a paintbrush to paint these watercolors on a sheet of white paper.
● **Dixie Cups** and **McCormick Food Coloring.** Pour one teaspoon water into a Dixie Cup and add three drops McCormick Food Coloring. Repeat in several Dixie Cups to make as many watercolors as you desire. Simply use a paintbrush to paint these watercolors on a sheet of white paper.

STRANGE FACTS
● On October 18, 1961, the New York Museum of Modern Art opened an exhibit of the works of French impressionist Henri Matisse, accidentally displaying one of the artist's paintings titled *Le Bateau* (The Boat) upside down for a total of 47 days. An estimated 116,000

Kool-Aid

Around 1918 in Hastings, Nebraska, twenty-five-year-old Edwin Perkins—having concocted flavoring extracts and perfumes, published a weekly newspaper, and served as postmaster—set up a mail order business called Perkins Products Co. to sell his concoctions through magazine advertisements.

One of Perkins' more popular products was a concentrated drink mix called Fruit Smack, available in six flavors at an economical price. Unfortunately, shipping the four-ounce glass bottles of syrup was costly, and the bottles frequently broke in the mail. In 1927, Perkins devised a method to dehydrate Fruit Smack so the resulting powder could be packaged in paper envelopes. He then designed and printed envelopes with the product's new name: Kool Ade (which would later become Kool-Aid).

The dramatic drop in postage costs enabled Perkins to wholesale Kool-Aid for ten cents a packet to stores. In 1929, he distributed Kool-Aid (available in strawberry, cherry, lemon-lime, grape, orange, and raspberry) through food brokers to grocery stores nationwide.

By 1931, the strong demand for Kool-Aid prompted Perkins to stop making his other products so he could devote all his attention to Kool-Aid. He moved the entire Kool-Aid operation to Chicago to streamline distribution. After World War II, Perkins enlarged the Kool-Aid factory, and by 1950, three hundred employees produced nearly a million packets of Kool-Aid every day.

In 1953, Perkins sold Kool-Aid to General Foods. Within a year, General Foods introduced a new advertising campaign for the drink mix, featuring the Smiling Face Pitcher, which has become an American icon. In 1989, General Foods merged with Kraft.

● During the Depression, Kool-Aid inventor Edwin Perkins cut the price of a packet of Kool-Aid in half to just five cents.

● In 1955, General Foods introduced root beer and lemonade flavored Kool-Aid.

● As of 2005, Kool-Aid was available in twenty flavors, with tropical punch as the most popular flavor, followed by lemonade, cherry, grape, and orange.

● Kool-Aid is the official soft drink of the state of Nebraska.

● Laid end to end, the number of packets of Kool-Aid sold in a year would stretch around the world twice.

museum visitors viewed the upside-down painting, including Matisse's son, Pierre. Wall Street stockbroker Genevieve Habert brought the mistake to the museum's attention—after visiting the exhibit for the third time.

● In his painting "Washington Crossing the Delaware," artist Emanuel Leutz depicts a United States flag that was not adopted by Congress until a year after Washington crossed the Delaware. Leutz also portrays the Durham boats Washington and his troops used as being approximately twenty feet long when they were actually forty to sixty feet long. He also incorrectly shows the soldiers holding their guns with the barrels pointed upward to catch the falling sleet.

● A painting of the *Last Supper* in the Cathedral on the northeast side of the Plaza de Armas in Cuzco, Peru, portrays Jesus and his disciples about to dine on an Inca delicacy—roast guinea pig.

● A youth group cleaning graffiti from the Mayrieres Cave near Brunquiel, France, wiped away part of a 15,000-year-old cave painting.

Paper

Marbled Paper
● **Gillette Foamy Shaving Cream** and **Forster Toothpicks.**
Spread a layer of Gillette Foamy Shaving Cream about one inch thick
onto a paper plate or a cookie sheet. Make the shaving cream level
by spreading it out using a piece of cardboard as a scraper. Using
tempera paint thinned with water, paint different shapes or patterns
on top of the layer of shaving cream. Using a Forster Toothpick, swirl
the paint on top of the shaving cream (without pushing it deep into
the shaving cream). Place a piece of white paper on top of the design,
press down lightly, and then remove the paper. Place the paper with
the shaving cream side up on a table, and use a piece of cardboard to
squeegee off the excess shaving cream. The marbled design remains
on the paper. Let dry. You can reuse the layer of shaving cream several
times, and then refresh when necessary.

● **Heinz White Vinegar, Crayola Chalk, Dixie Cups,** and
Wesson Vegetable Oil. Cover the kitchen counter with newspaper.
Fill a baking pan with water, add two tablespoons Heinz White
Vinegar, and place the pan in the middle of the newspaper. Using a
mortar and pestle, crush a piece of Crayola Chalk to a fine powder,
and then pour into a Dixie Cup. Repeat for all six pieces of chalk,
using a different cup for each piece. Add one tablespoon Wesson
Vegetable Oil to each cup, stirring thoroughly with a spoon. Pour the
contents of each paper cup into the pan of water. The chalky colored
oil will form large pools on the water's surface. Gently lay a piece of
white paper on the water's surface for a moment, lift off, and then
set to dry on a sheet of newspaper for twenty-four hours. When the
marbled paper dries, gently wipe off any surface chalk grains with a
paper towel. Swirling patterns of colored oil stick to the paper.

● **Dixie Cups** and **Sta-Flo Liquid Starch.** For each color you
wish to use, mix one tablespoon acrylic paint with two tablespoons
water in a Dixie Cup. Fill a cookie sheet or baking pan with one-half
cup Sta-Flo Liquid Starch. Add a few drops of several colors of your
prepared paint solutions. Using a paintbrush, a toothpick, or a wide-
tooth comb, swirl the colors in the pan. Place a sheet of white paper
on top of the colors for a moment, lift off, and then set to dry on a
sheet of newspaper for twenty-four hours. You can use the marbled
paper as stationery, wrapping paper, or to frame pictures.

Marbling Rake

● **Scotch Tape** and **Forster Toothpicks.** To make a wide-toothed
comb for swirling the colors in your marbling pan, use Scotch Tape to
tape several Forster Toothpicks about one inch apart along a piece of
corrugated cardboard.

Paper Bowls

● ***USA Today*, Kingsford's Corn Starch, Pam Cooking
Spray,** and **Aqua Net Hair Spray.** Cut sheets of *USA Today* into
long, thin strips (or feed the newspaper through a paper shredder)
until you have 1-1/2 cups of packed, shredded newspaper. Put the
shredded newspaper into a jar and fill it three quarters full of hot

tap water. Screw on the lid and let stand for three hours, shaking the jar occasionally and beating and stirring with a wooden spoon. As the paper absorbs the water, add more hot water. When the mixture becomes pasty and creamy, pour it into an electric blender. Dissolve three tablespoons Kingsford's Corn Starch in one-half cup hot water, pour into the blender, and blend—with adult supervision. Place the paper pulp in a sieve and strain the water from the pulp, pressing the pulp against the sides of the sieve to remove as much water as possible.

Spray a thin coat of Pam Cooking Spray along the inside of ceramic bowl. Press a thin layer of the pulp (approximately one-quarter-inch thick) against the inside of the bowl, covering the entire inside wall of the bowl. Let dry in a warm, dry area. When fully dry, separate the paper bowl from the ceramic bowl, using a butter knife, if necessary. Paint with colored paint, if desired. Spray the finished paper bowl with a thin coat of Aqua Net Hair Spray.

Recycled Papermaking

● ***USA Today*** and **Kingsford's Corn Starch.** Cut sheets of *USA Today* into long, thin strips (or feed the newspaper through a paper shredder) until you have 1-1/2 cups of packed, shredded newspaper. Put the shredded newspaper into a jar and fill it three quarters full of hot tap water. Screw on the lid and let stand for three hours, shaking the jar occasionally and beating and stirring with a wooden spoon. As the paper absorbs the water, add more hot water. When the mixture becomes pasty and creamy, pour it into an electric blender. Dissolve three tablespoons Kingsford's Corn Starch in one-half cup of hot water, pour into the blender, and blend—with adult supervision. Pour the mixture into a baking pan (larger than 8 x 10 inches). Place a metal screen (8 x 10 inches) on top of the mixture in the baking pan, and then gently push it down into the tray until the mixture covers it. Bring the screen up and place it on a sheet of newspaper and press it flat with the palm of your hand to squeeze away the water. Let the screen-backed paper mixture dry in the sun for several hours. When the paper is thoroughly dry, peel it from the screen backing and trim the edges with scissors.

- To add interesting specks to your homemade paper, after the paper pulp is blended, mix in colored confetti, small pieces of aluminum foil, tea leaves, flower petals, glitter, postage stamps, small colored threads, or snips of ribbon.
- To make scented paper, add a few drops of your favorite perfume to the paper pulp and blend thoroughly.
- To make colored paper, add a few drops of McCormick Food Coloring to the paper pulp and blend well.
- You can make different batches of paper pulp in different colors and then press them together to make colorful objects.
- You can make a gift bag by simply marbling the face of a white paper bag.
- To make colorful stationery, marble the face of a white envelope.
- Make postcards or bookmarks by marbling the unlined side of white index cards.

STRANGE FACTS

- Before the advent of paper, most documents were written on parchment (made from the skin of sheep or goats) or vellum (made from the skin of calves). A single book three hundred pages long would require the skins of an estimated eighteen sheep.
- The first paper, invented in China in 105 C.E. by Ts'ai Lun, the Emperor Ho-Ti's minister of public works, was made from the inner bark of the mulberry tree, fishnets, old rags, and waste hemp.
- Marbling paper was practiced in Japan and China as early as the twelfth century. According to a Japanese legend, the gods gave knowledge of the marbling process to a man named Jiyemon Hiroba as a reward for his devotion to the Katsuga Shrine.
- For centuries, paper marbling masters worked in secrecy to maintain a shroud of mystery to prevent others from mastering the craft and going into business for themselves.

● The watermark was discovered by accident. In 1282, a small piece of wire caught in the paper press being used at the Fabrino Paper Mill made a line in the finished paper that could be seen by holding the paper up to the light. The papermakers realized a design made from wire would create a decorative watermark, which could also be used on banknotes to thwart counterfeiters.

● For hundreds of years, paper was made by hand from the pulp of rags. Rag pulp is still used today to make most high-quality bond paper.

● Benjamin Franklin purchased used rags for paper mills. At the time, most paper was made from worn-out clothes made from cotton and linen.

● Early umbrellas were made from paper coated with oil to make them waterproof.

● Paper can be made inexpensively from hemp. However, in 1937, cotton growers, fearing competition from hemp growers, lobbied against marijuana (the dried leaves of the hemp plant) to make hemp illegal. In 1999, Governor Jesse "The Body" Ventura signed legislation making hemp farming legal in Minnesota.

● Toilet paper and facial tissues are made from wood pulp treated with plant resins to make it absorbent.

● The average American uses 640 pounds of paper and paperboard every year.

● Money is made out of cotton, not paper.

Papier-Mâché

Fabric Stiffener
● **Elmer's Glue-All** and *USA Today.* Mix water and Elmer's Glue-All in a bowl to the desired consistency. Strips of newspaper or fabric dipped in the mixture can be shaped and dried in decorative forms and shapes.

Papier-Mâché Formulas
● **Gold Medal Flour, *USA Today*, and Elmer's Glue-All.** Mix one cup Gold Medal Flour with two-thirds cup water in a medium-size bowl to a thick-glue consistency. To thicken, add more flour. Cut *USA Today* into strips approximately one to two inches in width. Dip each strip into the paste, gently pull it between your fingers to remove excess paste, and apply it to any object (an empty bottle, carton, or canister). Repeat over the surface you want to cover. Let dry, and then decorate with poster paint. After the paint dries, mix equal parts Elmer's Glue-All and water, and paint your finished papier-mâché project with a coat of the mixture to seal it and give it a glossy shine.

● **Gold Medal Flour, C&H Sugar, *USA Today*, and Elmer's Glue-All.** Mix one-half cup Gold Medal Flour, two tablespoons C&H

Sugar, and two cups water in a pot. With adult supervision, bring the mixture to a boil over medium heat, stirring constantly. Lower heat, simmer, and stir until the mixture thickens. Cut *USA Today* into strips approximately one to two inches in width. Dip each strip into the paste, gently pull it between your fingers to remove excess paste, and apply it to any object (an empty bottle, carton, or canister). Repeat over the surface you want to cover. Continue until the base is completely covered. Let dry, and then decorate with poster paint. After the paint dries, mix equal parts Elmer's Glue-All and water and paint your finished papier-mâché project with a coat of the mixture to seal it and give it a glossy shine.

● **Kleenex Tissues** and **Sta-Flo Liquid Starch.** Tear several Kleenex Tissues into small pieces, place in a large bowl, and pour in just enough Sta-Flo Liquid Starch to wet the paper. Press the tissue paper together to form a small ball, squeezing out the excess liquid. Mold the mash into any shape you wish, let dry, and then paint.

Sealant

● **Aqua Net Hair Spray.** Spray your finished papier-mâché project with a thin coat of Aqua Net Hair Spray to seal it and give it a glossy shine.

Textures

● **Hartz Parakeet Seed** and **Elmer's Glue-All.** Attach Hartz Parakeet Seed with Elmer's Glue-All to your finished papier-mâché project to add texture. Add the bird seed before painting your project.

● **Kleenex Tissues.** Use Kleenex Tissues as the paper for your papier-mâché projects to achieve different textures.

● **Oral-B Dental Floss** and **Elmer's Glue-All.** Attach Oral-B Dental Floss, coiled into pleasing shapes, with Elmer's Glue-All to your finished papier-mâché project to add texture. You can add the dental floss before or after painting your project, depending whether you wish to utilize the natural color of the floss.

● **Uncle Ben's Converted Brand Rice** and **Elmer's Glue-All.** Adhere uncooked Uncle Ben's Converted Brand Rice with Elmer's Glue-All to your finished papier-mâché project to add texture. You

● You can make a form on which to build your papier-mâché sculpture from inflated balloons, chicken wire, cardboard boxes, toilet-paper tubes, empty cereal boxes, empty milk cartons, empty toothpaste boxes, a clothes hanger, or crumpled aluminum foil or paper.

● Add small torn pieces of colored construction paper to your papier-mâché paste to create small specks of color.

can add the rice before or after painting your project, depending whether you wish to utilize the natural color of the rice.

STRANGE FACTS

● The phrase papier-mâché is French for "mashed paper," despite the fact that the craft was invented by the Chinese.

● The Chinese developed paper during the Han Dynasty (circa 202 B.C.E.– 220 C.E.), and archeologists have identified artifacts made from papier-mâché from this period.

● The ancient Chinese made battle helmets from paper-mâché strengthened with several coats of lacquer.

● Paper-mâché has been used to make dolls, toys, furniture, trays, screens, buttons, tableware, snuff boxes, and candy containers.

● Female wasps build nests out of papier-mâché. The wasps chew old wood and tough plant fibers to pulp, using much saliva. The insects shape this pulp into a nest of hexagon-shaped cells that hang from a plant stem or an awning. Each cell generally holds one egg.

Potpourri

● **Bounce.** Fill a clean, used Bounce sheet with either fresh coffee or potpourri, gather up the edges, and tie with a ribbon.

● **L'eggs Sheer Energy Panty Hose.** Cut off the foot from a clean, used pair of L'eggs Sheer Energy Panty Hose, fill with rose petals from your flower bed, and tie a knot in the nylon. Set the sachet on a tabletop or place it in a drawer.

● **L'eggs Sheer Energy Panty Hose** and **Lipton Chamomile Tea Bags.** Cut off the foot from a clean, used pair of L'eggs Sheer Energy Panty Hose, fill with the tea leaves from six Lipton Chamomile Tea Bags, and tie a knot in the nylon. Set the sachet on a tabletop, place it in a drawer, or hang it from a lamp.

● **L'eggs Sheer Energy Panty Hose** and **Maxwell House Coffee.** Cut off the foot from a clean, used pair of L'eggs Sheer Energy Panty Hose, fill with Maxwell House Coffee grounds, and tie a knot in the nylon. Keep the sachet on your night table or desk.

● **Morton Kosher Salt.** To make moist potpourri for filling sachets, place a layer of fragrant leaves and flowers in the bottom of a glass bowl. Cover with Morton Kosher Salt (which is more coarse than regular salt). Place a second layer of leaves and flowers on top of the salt and cover with more salt. Repeat until you have used all the plant materials. Cover the top layer of salt with a flat dish and place a weight on top of it. Set in a dry place undisturbed for approximately three weeks or until the salt thickens and cakes. Add essential oils and a fixative (if desired) and mix with a wooden spoon. Cover the bowl and store in a cool dark place for six months to age the potpourri.

● **Quaker Oats, McCormick Vanilla Extract,** and **L'eggs Sheer Energy Panty Hose.** Mix one cup Quaker Oats with one teaspoon McCormick Vanilla Extract. Cut off the foot from a clean, used pair of L'eggs Sheer Energy Panty Hose, fill with the vanilla-scented Quaker Oats, and tie a knot in the nylon. Set the sachet on a tabletop, place it in a drawer, or hang it from a lamp.

● **Ziploc Storage Bags.** To make potpourri, collect dried roses, juniper sprigs, tiny pinecones, strips of orange rind, bay leaves, cinnamon sticks, whole cloves, and allspice berries. Mix a few drops of rose, cinnamon, and balsam oils with orrisroot (available at your local crafts store). Add all ingredients and seal in a Ziploc Storage Bag for a few weeks to mellow, turning the bag occasionally.

STRANGE FACTS

● During medieval times, people created potpourri by placing flowers, herbs, and spices in jars, adding salt to pickle and preserve the ingredients, sealing the containers securely, and leaving them sit until the contents rotted. They used the resulting pungent concoction to perfume the air in castles and homes that lacked indoor plumbing.

● The word *potpourri* is French for "rotten pot."

● For thousands of years, cultures around the world have used the fragrances of flowers, spices, and herbs to enhance ceremonies, create a romantic atmosphere, and freshen the air in stuffy rooms.

● In sixteenth-century England, Queen Elizabeth created the official royal position of Herb Strewer and Potpourri Maker, which was discontinued in the twentieth century during the reign of Queen Elizabeth II.

● Potpourri makers eventually figured out that open bowls of dried flowers and herbs created more pleasing scents than potpourri pots.

Sand Art

Colored Macaroni
● **McCormick Food Coloring, Kraft Macaroni & Cheese, Reynolds Cut-Rite Wax Paper,** and **Elmer's Glue-All.** Add a few drops of McCormick Food Coloring to a bowl of water. Dip dry Kraft Macaroni & Cheese noodles in the water and drain. Place the colored noodles on a sheet of Reynolds Cut-Rite Wax Paper and let dry. Use Elmer's Glue-All to glue the colored pasta to a sheet of construction paper, or any object you wish to decorate with texture.

Colored Rice
● **McCormick Food Coloring, Heinz White Vinegar, Uncle Ben's Converted Brand Rice,** *USA Today*, **Ziploc Storage Bags,** and **Elmer's Glue-All.** Mix several drops of McCormick Food Coloring and one-quarter cup Heinz White Vinegar in a clean, empty jar. Pour one-half cup uncooked Uncle Ben's Converted Brand Rice into the jar, screw on the lid securely, and shake the jar until the rice is evenly colored. Let sit for five minutes. Using a sieve, strain the liquid from the rice. Spread the colored rice on a section of *USA Today* newspaper and set in the sun to dry. Store the colored rice in an airtight container or a Ziploc Storage Bag. Repeat to make other colors. Colored rice makes an excellent nontoxic alternative to glitter and colored sand. Adhere to art project with Elmer's Glue-All.

Colored Salt
● **Morton Salt, Rubbermaid, McCormick Food Coloring,** and **Elmer's Glue-All.** Pour one-half cup Morton Salt into a Rubbermaid container, add a few drops of McCormick Food Coloring, and stir with a spoon until the salt is evenly colored. Set the container in a warm, dry place. Occasionally stir the salt with a

spoon to bring the damp salt to the surface. Repeat to make other colors. Store in the airtight container. Colored rice makes an excellent nontoxic alternative to glitter and colored sand. Adhere to art projects with Elmer's Glue-All.

Froot Loop Art
● **Elmer's Glue-All** and **Kellogg's Froot Loops.** On a sheet of paper, draw a design using Elmer's Glue-All and glue colored Froot Loops to the paper to color your design.

Froot Loops Bottle Art
● **Kellogg's Froot Loops, Ziploc Storage Bags,** and **Miracle Whip jar.** Sort a box of Kellogg's Froot Loops by color, place each color in its own Ziploc Storage Bag, and seal each bag closed, leaving as little air as possible in each bag. Using a rolling pin or your hands, crush the Froot Loops in each bag into powder. Layer different colors of crushed Froot Loops into a clean, empty Miracle Whip jar, and then screw on the lid, sealing tightly.

Jell-O Sand Art
● **Jell-O** and **Forster Toothpicks.** Divide a box of Jell-O powder among four clear, plastic cups. Repeat with a second, third, and fourth color, until you have four cups with four layers of different colors of powder. Insert a Forster Toothpick along the inside of the plastic cup, gently poking to create color patterns. When you remove the toothpick, the layers of color will cross into each other. After admiring your sand art, prepare each cup of Jell-O according to the directions on the box.

Kool-Aid Sand Bottles
● **Kool-Aid, Gerber Baby Food,** and **Forster Toothpicks.** Pour a layer of a brightly colored Kool-Aid drink mix powder into a clean, empty Gerber Baby Food jar. Add more layers of color with different

colors of Kool-Aid powder. Insert a Forster Toothpick along the inside of the jar, gently poking to create color patterns. When you remove the toothpick, the layers of color will cross into each other. With adult supervision, put hot glue around the lip of the jar and screw the lid on the jar securely.

Popcorn Art
● **Orville Redenbacher's Gourmet Popping Corn, Dixie Cups, McCormick Food Coloring, Bounty Paper Towels,** and **Elmer's Glue-All.** Have an adult help you pop some Orville Redenbacher's Gourmet Popping Corn (without butter flavoring). Fill several Dixie Cups with water and add a few drops of a different colored McCormick Food Coloring to each one. Add a few pieces of popcorn to each cup of colored water, stir with a spoon, and quickly remove the popcorn, placing the pieces on a sheet of Bounty Paper Towels to dry. Let dry overnight. On a sheet of paper, draw a design using Elmer's Glue-All and glue the colored popcorn to the paper to color your design. Let dry overnight.

Rice Paintings
● **McCormick Food Coloring, Heinz White Vinegar, Uncle Ben's Converted Brand Rice,** *USA Today*, **Elmer's Glue-All,** and **Dixie Cups.** Mix several drops of McCormick Food Coloring and one-quarter cup Heinz White Vinegar in a clean, empty jar. Pour one-half cup uncooked Uncle Ben's Converted Brand Rice into the jar, screw on the lid securely, and shake the jar until the rice is evenly colored. Let sit for five minutes. Using a sieve, strain the liquid from the rice. Spread the colored rice on a section of *USA Today* newspaper and set in the sun to dry. Store the colored rice in an airtight container or a Ziploc Storage Bag. Repeat to make other colors.

Mix one teaspoon Elmer's Glue-All and one teaspoon water in a Dixie Cup. Using a pencil, lightly draw your design on a piece of paper. Use a paintbrush to paint the watery glue solution over whichever area you intend to be your first color. Sprinkle the colored rice over the glue, let dry, and then gently shake off the excess rice. Repeat for each color you wish to use.

Salt (or Rice) Sand Bottles

● **Gerber Baby Food, Forster Toothpicks,** and **Scotch Packaging Tape.** Using a variety of colored salt or colored rice (see "Colored Salt" on page 109 or "Colored Rice" on page 109), make a three-dimensional painting in a clean, empty jar of Gerber Baby Food. Spoon a layer of colored salt or rice into the jar. Make the layer level or tilted, varying the height of each layer as your prefer. Add a second layer using a different color salt or rice, repeating until you reach the top of the jar. To make designs in the bands of color, push a Forster Toothpick inside the jar, along the side of the glass through the layers of colored salt or rice. When you remove the toothpick, the layers of color will cross into each other. Screw the lid on the jar and seal with Scotch Packing Tape (to prevent the lid from opening accidentally and spilling forth salt or rice).

STRANGE FACTS

● During the seventeenth century, the Pueblo people embraced sand painting as a spiritual art form, and the practice spread westward to the Navajos, Apaches, Tohono O'odhams (Papagos), Zunis, and tribes in what is today southern California.

● Today the Navajos are the most dynamic practitioners of sand painting, which remains an important part of their ceremonial life.

● To create sand paintings, Native Americans traditionally use sands of natural colors, cornmeal, flower and corn pollen, and powdered roots and bark. The artist, chanting during a Navajo religious healing ceremony, sprinkles these materials on the ground to temporarily form sacred symbols and representations of supernatural beings—to unite the past, present, and future into a single moment of time in the universe.

● Native Americans who practice traditional sand painting refuse to make their sand paintings permanent—to prevent the supernatural power generated by the designs from causing any harm.

Science Fun

Alka-Seltzer Rocket
● **Fuji 35 mm Film, Scotch Tape,** and **Alka-Seltzer.** On Fuji
35 mm film canisters, the lid snaps inside the body. Roll a sheet of
construction paper or wrapping paper around the film canister, so the
open end of the film canister sticks out.
Tape the paper onto the film canister.
With adult supervision, use a pair of
scissors and Scotch Tape to add a paper
cone to the top of the paper tube. Hold
the rocket upside down so the open end
of the film canister faces upward. Fill
the canister halfway with cold tap water.
Drop in two Alka-Seltzer tablets. Snap
on the lid, turn the rocket right side
up, set it down on the ground, and
quickly step back. The rocket blasts
approximately six feet off the ground.

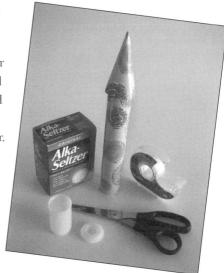

Disappearing Chalk
● **Heinz White Vinegar** and **Crayola Chalk.**
Pour one cup Heinz White Vinegar into a clean, empty jar, drop in
one stick of Crayola Chalk, and observe for ten minutes. Bubbles
rise from the stick of chalk, which soon breaks into small pieces and
dissolves completely. The acetic acid in the vinegar dissolves the
calcium carbonate in the chalk, releasing carbon dioxide gas.

Floating Egg
● **Morton Salt.** Fill a clean, empty jar halfway with hot tap water.
Stir in one tablespoon Morton Salt at a time until no more salt will

dissolve in the water. Gently drop an uncooked egg into the salt water. The egg floats in the water. Now slowly pour regular tap water over the egg, filling up the rest of the jar. The egg floats on top of the salt water, but it remains under the layer of regular tap water.

Flying Ping-Pong Ball
● **Conair Pro Styler 1600 Hair Dryer.** With adult supervision, plug in the hair dryer, turn it on "high cool," and aim the nozzle straight up in the air. Hold a Ping-Pong ball directly over the nozzle and gently release the ball. The Ping-Pong ball hovers upward in the middle of the airstream and stays in place, as if floating on a cushion of air. You can also tilt the blow dryer roughly twenty degrees and the Ping-Pong ball will remaining floating.

Invisible Ink
● **Q-Tips Cotton Swabs** and **ReaLemon.** Use a Q-Tips Cotton Swab as a pen to write in ReaLemon on a piece of white paper. Let dry at room temperature. The letters will disappear. With adult supervision, iron the piece of paper. The writing will turn brown.

Jell-O Garden
● **Jell-O.** Mix up Jell-O according to the instructions, pour the gelatin into several clear plastic drinking cups, and let harden in the refrigerator. Place the cups of hardened gelatin on the counter and push several sunflower seeds into the center of the surface of the Jell-O, pushing them down approximately the length of your finger. Let the jar of gelatin stand on a counter near a window to get light. Do not water. Observe. The seeds grow in the Jell-O, enabling you to observe the root structures and the seedling sprouts. The Jell-O may also grow a thin, harmless mold on the surface.

Lava Lamp
● **Canada Dry Club Soda** and **Sun-Maid Raisins.** To make a poor man's lava lamp, fill a glass with Canada Dry Club Soda and drop in four or five Sun-Maid Raisins. The carbonation will cause the raisins to repeatedly bob to the surface and then sink again.

Magic Salt Crystal Garden

● **Kingsford's Charcoal Briquets, Morton Salt, Mrs. Stewart's Liquid Bluing, Parsons' Ammonia,** and **McCormick Food Coloring.** With a hammer, break up five charcoal briquets into one-inch chunks. Place the pieces in the bottom of a two-quart glass bowl. In a clean, empty jar, mix six tablespoons Morton Salt, six tablespoons Mrs. Stewart's Liquid Bluing, one tablespoon Parsons' Ammonia, and two tablespoons water. Pour the mixture over the charcoal in the bowl. Sprinkle a few drops of McCormick Food Coloring over each piece of charcoal. Let the bowl sit undisturbed in a safe place for seventy-two hours. Fluffy, fragile crystals will form on top of the charcoal, and some will climb up the sides of the bowl. The salt recrystallizes into beautiful, delicate coral-like formations. As the ammonia speeds up the evaporation of the water, the blue ion particles in the bluing and the salt get carried up into the porous charcoal, where the salt crystallizes around the blue particles as nuclei. These crystals are porous like a sponge, and the liquid below continues to move into the openings and evaporate, leaving layers of crystals. To keep the crystals growing, add another batch of ammonia, salt, bluing, and water.

Poor Man's Telephone

● **Dixie Cups.** Punch a small hole in the bottom of two Dixie Cups. Then thread the ends of a long piece of string through the holes and tie each end to a button. You and a friend each take a cup and walk apart until the string is straight and taut. Speak into the open end of your cup. Your sound waves travel along the string and can be heard by your friend through the open end of the other cup.

● **Campbell's Soup.** With adult supervision, use a hammer and a nail to punch a small hole in the bottom of two clean, empty Campbell's Soup cans. Then thread the ends of a long piece of string through the holes and tie each end to a button. You and a friend each take a can and walk apart until the string is straight and taut. Speak into the open end of your can. Your sound waves travel along the string and can be heard by your friend through the open end of the other can.

Potato, Sweet Potato, or Avocado

● **Forster Toothpicks.** To get a potato, sweet potato, or avocado seed to sprout roots and leaves, insert four Forster Toothpicks securely and equidistantly around the equator of the potato, sweet potato, or avocado seed . (You can use a nail to punch starter holes in the avocado seed.) Fill a glass with water and set the potato or avocado seed in the glass so the toothpicks allow only the bottom half of the potato or avocado seed to sit in the water. Place the glass on a window ledge to get sunlight. When roots and shoots appear, pot the plant in soil.

Reflection Card

● **Reynolds Wrap** and **Elmer's Glue-All.** Paint one side of a piece of cardboard black (or glue a sheet of black construction paper to the cardboard). With adult supervision, use a pair of scissors to cut out any assortment of shapes (circles, squares, triangles, long strips, random polygons) from a sheet of Reynolds Wrap—without crinkling the aluminum foil. Use Elmer's Glue-All to glue the shapes (shiny side up) to the black side of the cardboard. Let dry.

To use, hold the reflection card under bright light from the sun or a lamp, angling the card so the light reflects onto a wall, ceiling, object, or person. Experiment with different designs.

Rubber Chicken Bone

● **Heinz White Vinegar.** Turn a chicken bone into "rubber" by soaking a clean chicken bone in a glass of Heinz Vinegar for seven days. After that, the chicken bone will bend like rubber. It can be twisted, and, in some cases, tied in a knot. The vinegar (acetic acid) dissolves the calcium from the bone, leaving it soft and bendable.

Rubber Egg

● **Heinz White Vinegar.** Place a hard-boiled egg in a clean, empty glass jar. Cover with vinegar. Secure the lid and let the jar stand for seven days. The eggshell dissolves, and you are left with a rubbery egg that will actually bounce if not dropped from too great a height. The acetic acid in the vinegar dissolves the calcium carbonate in the eggshell.

Steel Wool Sparkler

● **S.O.S Steel Wool Pad** and **Energizer 9-volt battery.** With adult supervision, pull the S.O.S Steel Wool Pad apart until it is the size of a tennis ball. Place the steel wool pad in a baking pan. Touch the ends of the Energizer 9-volt battery to the steel wool. The sparks from the battery cause the steel wool to catch on fire, and the iron filings from the steel wool sparkle like a Fourth of July sparkler.

Underwater Fireworks

● **Wesson Vegetable Oil, Dixie Cups,** and **McCormick Food Coloring.** Fill a large, clear glass bowl with water. Pour one tablespoon Wesson Vegetable Oil into each of four Dixie Cups. Add four drops of McCormick Food Coloring to a cup and repeat with the other colors for the other cups Mix the oil and colors thoroughly with the spoon. Pour the colored oil mixture into the water in the bowl. Observe as small pools of oil spotted with tiny spheres of color float to the surface of the water, exploding outward and creating flat circles of color on the surface of the water. Long streamers of color then sink down through the water, like a fireworks display.

Oil and water are *immiscible*—meaning they do not mix, but separate into layers because of the different polarity of their molecules. The oil rises to the surface because it is less dense than the water. Since the water-based food coloring does not dissolve in oil, it remains in tiny spheres throughout the oil on the water's surface, and then sinks through the oil layer and dissolves in the water below, creating long streamers of color.

Volcano

● **Coca-Cola, Arm & Hammer Baking Soda, Dawn Dishwashing Liquid, McCormick Food Coloring,** and **Heinz White Vinegar.** Place a clean, empty, two-liter Coca-Cola bottle on the bottom of a kitchen sink, bathtub, or shower floor. Using a funnel, pour one cup water into the bottle. Add one tablespoon Arm & Hammer Baking Soda, one tablespoon Dawn Dishwashing Liquid, and ten drops red McCormick Food Coloring. Pour one cup Heinz White Vinegar into the bottle and scream "Volcano! Volcano! Volcano!" Red foam "lava" will bubble out the top of the volcano and down the sides of the bottle.

STRANGE FACTS

● On January 13, 1920, the *New York Times* editorialized that rocket scientist Robert H. Goddard "does not know the relation of action to reaction, and of the need to have something better than a vacuum against which to react—to say that would be absurd. Of course he only seems to lack the knowledge ladled out daily in high schools. . . ." On July 17, 1969, three days before *Apollo 11* landed on the moon, the *New York Times* retracted the statement.

● If the Spaceship Earth geodesic sphere at EPCOT were a golf ball, to be the proportional size to hit it, you'd be two miles tall.

● Hydrogen is used as rocket fuel because the combustion reaction between hydrogen and oxygen propels the exhaust gas (primarily water vapor) out of the rocket's engine at 7910 miles per hour— creating enormous thrust to lift the 4.4 million-pound space shuttle into orbit.

● In most science fiction movies, the rockets on spacecraft make violent roaring sounds and explosions as they travel through space. In reality, spacecraft do not make any sounds in space, since space is a vacuum.

Sculpture

Ice Sculptures

● **McCormick Food Coloring.** To make colorful ice sculpture, fill buckets, dishpans, and other containers with water, add a few drops of McCormick Food Coloring, and leave outside overnight in freezing weather. Remove the ice from the molds and build a colored miniature version of Stonehenge in your yard. Or fill an ice-cube tray with colored water, freeze into ice cubes, and use to build colorful miniature igloos.

Soap Carving

● **Ivory Soap** and **Forster Toothpicks.** Unwrap a bar of Ivory Soap. For best results, let the bar of soap dry for 24 hours before carving. With adult supervision, use a paring knife to cut away the raised edges and scrape off the lettering. If you know what shape or design you intend to carve, you can carve directly in the soap, or use a Forster Toothpick stick to outline a rough sketch on the soap. You can also sketch your idea on a piece of paper and then transfer it to the soap. Using the paring knife, cut off the small pieces of soap that will not be a part of your design, leaving roughly a one-quarter-inch margin around your outline to allow for more detailed work later. When you finish carving, let the soap dry for a day or two. Then polish the sculpture by rubbing it with a soft paper napkin. Your carving will float in a bathtub full of water, so consider carving boats, turtles, or other sea creatures for more fun.

SPAM Carving

● **SPAM.** Remove a block of SPAM from the can and, with adult supervision, use a paring knife to carefully carve the block of luncheon meat into whatever your heart desires (Mount Rushmore, farm animals, a race car, the Statue of Liberty, etc.).

3-D Pictures

● **Gold Medal Flour, Morton Salt,** and **Forster Toothpicks.** Mix two cups Gold Medal Flour and one cup Morton Salt in a bowl, and then add one cup water and blend thoroughly. Knead until the dough is smooth. If the dough is too loose, add more flour. If the dough is too firm, add more water. Dampen a piece of cardboard, and then roll out a thin layer of flour dough on the cardboard for the background. Using a Forster Toothpick, sketch out your picture. Roll out more dough and cut out various shapes to press into the background wherever you wish. Let dry overnight or longer, if necessary. Then paint, if you wish.

STRANGE FACTS

● Seattle, Washington, holds a yearly SPAM carving contest. Each contestant is given one can of SPAM and fifteen minutes to carve it into anything they like (cars, animals, people's faces, etc.).

● The statue of Ecuador's renowned poet José Olmedo in the city of Guayaquil is actually a statue of English poet Lord Byron. The city of Guayaquil, unable to afford to commission a sculptor, purchased the statue of Byron from a London junk dealer and changed the plaque to read "José Olmedo."

● Adhering to a mistranslated passage in the Bible stating that "horns" (rather than "rays of light") emanated from the head of Moses when he descended from Mount Sinai carrying the ten commandments, Michelangelo sculpted Moses the Lawgiver with horns on Moses' head—proliferating the false notion that Jews had horns and further fueling anti-Semitism.

● The word bones is slang for "dice," which were originally carved from bones.

● Around 800 B.C.E., the Etruscans (the people living in the region known today as Tuscany, Italy) invented dentures, carving individual teeth from ivory, molding bridgework from gold, and extracting teeth from the dead to make dentures for the wealthy.

● In 1935, during a exhibition of Van Gogh's paintings at New York's Museum of Modern Art, prankster Hugh Troy hung on the wall a velvet-lined shadow box that contained a piece of dried beef that he had carved into the shape of an ear with a sign that read, "This is the ear that Van Gogh cut off and sent to his mistress Dec. 24, 1888."

Slime

Freaky Foam
● **Gillette Foamy Shaving Cream** and **Elmer's Glue-All.**

Using a spoon, mix one cup Gillette Foamy Shaving Cream and the contents of one four-ounce bottle of Elmer's Glue-All in a mixing bowl. With the spoon, whip the glue and shaving cream together. Mold whatever you want out of the mixture. Let set overnight to dry. The mixture solidifies into foam.

Whipping the shaving cream and the glue together essentially fills the polyvinyl acetate molecules in the glue with air-filled soap lather. The glue dries filled with millions of tiny cells of air, much like foam rubber.

Green Slime
● **Elmer's Glue-All, McCormick Food Coloring,** and **20 Mule Team Borax.**

In a large bowl, mix two cups Elmer's Glue-All with 1-1/2 cups water and twenty drops McCormick Food Coloring. In a second bowl, mix one teaspoon 20 Mule Team Borax with one-third cup water. Add the second bowl to the first bowl and mix until it clumps, and then take out the clump and set aside. Make another bowl of borax and water and again add it to the first bowl. Take out the clump and set aside. Repeat this process until the glue solution in the first bowl is gone. Makes three to four small clumps of green slime. Store in an airtight container. The resulting soft, pliable, rubbery glob snaps if pulled quickly, stretches if pulled slowly, and slowly oozes to the floor if placed over the edge of a table.

Nutty Putty

● **Sta-Flo Liquid Starch, Elmer's Glue-All, McCormick Food Coloring** (optional), and **Ziploc Storage Bag.** Mix one-half cup Sta-Flo Liquid Starch and one-half cup Elmer's Glue-All until you achieve the consistency of putty. If desired, add a few drops of McCormick Food Coloring. Store in an airtight container or a Ziploc Storage Bag, and refrigerate. (Be sure to use Elmer's Glue-All, not Elmer's School Glue.)

Quicksand

● **Kingsford's Corn Starch.** Cover the tabletop with newspaper. Combine 1-1/4 cups Kingsford's Corn Starch and one cup water in a large bowl and stir until the mixture looks like a thick and sticky paste. Make a fist and pound on the surface of the quicksand. Then lightly push your fingers down into the mixture. When you hit the surface of the mixture with your fist, the quicksand supports your weight, but when you push your fingers into the mixture, they easily sink to the bottom of the bowl.

STRANGE FACTS

● Green Slime is a non-Newtonian fluid—a liquid that does not abide by any of Sir Isaac Newton's laws on how liquids behave. Quicksand, gelatin, and ketchup are all non-Newtonian fluids.

● A non-Newtonian fluid's ability to flow can be changed by applying a force. Pushing or pulling on the slime makes it temporarily thicker and less oozy.

● The 1984 movie *Ghostbusters*, starring Bill Murray, Dan Aykroyd, Sigourney Weaver, and Harold Ramis, and featuring ghosts that spewed slime, inspired the catchphrase "I've been slimed."

● At the end of the Nickelodeon game show *Double Dare*, the members of the winning team get buckets of green slime dumped on them.

Tie-Dyeing

● **Kool-Aid, Heinz White Vinegar,** and **Playtex Living Gloves.** For each color you wish to use, mix the contents of one package of Kool-Aid and one ounce Heinz White Vinegar in individual plastic bowls until dissolved. Using rubber bands, pull and twist a white T-shirt (that has not been prewashed using fabric softener) into different shapes. Wearing Playtex Living Gloves, dip the rubber-banded ends in the bowls. To set colors, with adult supervision, iron on medium-high placing an ironing cloth between the shirt and the iron. Let set for 24 hours before washing. To avoid running colors, wash separately the first time. Launder T-shirt as usual, and it's ready to wear.

Other Fabric Dyes

● **Lipton Tea Bags** and **Playtex Living Gloves.** Brew a pot of really strong tea, using several Lipton Tea Bags. Wearing Playtex Living Gloves, submerge the garment into the hot tea. Let dry.

● **Maxwell House Coffee, Rubbermaid,** and **Playtex Living Gloves.** With adult supervision, brew two pots of Maxwell House Coffee and pour into a larger Rubbermaid container. Wearing Playtex Living Gloves, dip the cloth into the hot coffee. Let dry.

● **Mrs. Stewart's Liquid Bluing.** In a bucket, mix one tablespoon Mrs. Stewart's Liquid Bluing in one gallon of water. Wrap rubber bands around sections of a white T-shirt, submerge the T-shirt into the mixture in the bucket, wring well, let dry, and then remove the rubber bands.

● **Tang, Heinz White Vinegar,** and **Playtex Living Gloves.** Mix one-half cup Tang powdered mix and one ounce Heinz White Vinegar in a bowl until dissolved. Wearing Playtex Living Gloves, submerge the garment into the orange solution. To set colors, with adult supervision iron the cloth of garment on medium-high, placing an ironing cloth between the cloth and the iron. Let set for 24 hours before washing. To avoid running colors, wash separately the first time.

● **Welch's 100% Purple Grape Juice** and **Playtex Living Gloves.** Pour one cup Welch's 100% Purple Grape Juice into a bowl. Wearing Playtex Living Gloves, dip the T-shirt into the grape juice. To set colors, with adult supervision iron the cloth of garment on medium-high, placing an ironing cloth between the cloth and the iron. Let set for 24 hours before washing. To avoid running colors, wash separately the first time.

Reverse Tie Dye

● **Clorox Bleach.** With adult supervision, mix two cups Clorox Bleach in a bucket of hot water. Use traditional tie-dying techniques (rubber bands or string) to prepare a dark-colored T-shirt. Place the shirt in the bleach solution, stirring occasionally until the color of the shirt lightens considerably. Remove the rubber bands or string and dry as usual. Launder the shirt in the washing machine with your regular detergent.

STRANGE FACTS

● Contrary to popular belief, tie-dyeing was not invented by the counterculture in the 1960s in the United States. The earliest surviving examples of tie-dyed fabric are pre-Columbian alpaca, found in Peru and dating from the first and second centuries B.C.E.

● Tie-dyed silks dating from the Tang Dynasty (618–906 C.E.) have been discovered in the burial grounds at Astana and Khotan on the Old Silk Road in Sin Kiang, East Turkistan.

Towers and Bridges

Dixie Cup Bridge

● **Dixie Cups.** To build this bridge, you will need seventy-five five-ounce Dixie Cups and three sheets of corrugated cardboard (roughly sixteen-by-sixteen inches wide). Place twenty-five paper cups upside down on the floor in five rows of five cups each. Place the first sheet of cardboard on top of the cups. Place another twenty-five paper cups upside down on top of the cardboard in five rows of five cups each. Place the second sheet of cardboard on top of the cups. Place the last twenty-five paper cups upside down on top of the cardboard in five rows of five cups each. Place the third sheet of cardboard on top of the cups. With adult supervision, slowly step on top of the cardboard. The paper cups support your weight.

Each paper cup is a cylinder, capable of supporting up to sixteen pounds of weight. The sheets of cardboard help spread the weight equally across all the cups underneath.

Green Pea Tower

● **Birds Eye Baby Peas** and **Forster Toothpicks.** Pour a bag of Birds Eye Baby Peas into a bowl and fill the bowl with warm water, covering the peas by at least an inch. Let soak overnight. Drain the water from the peas. Insert the end of a Forster Toothpick into a pea, and then connect another toothpick to the pea, constructing bridges, tunnels, or whatever you wish to design. When finished, set aside to let the peas dry out, forming tight connectors for the toothpicks.

Marshmallow Tower
● **Jet-Puffed Miniature Marshmallows** and **Forster Toothpicks.** Construct buildings, bridges, and towers using only Jet-Puffed Miniature Marshmallows and Forster Toothpicks.

Shaving Cream Tower
● **Dixie Cups, Gillette Foamy Shaving Cream, Forster Toothpicks,** and **Glad Drinking Straws.** Give you and your friends ten minutes to see which kid can build the tallest structure using only an eight-ounce Dixie Cup filled with Gillette Foamy Shaving Cream, fifty Forster Toothpicks, and six Glad Drinking Straws. The Dixie Cup may be used as part of the structure, and the tower must stand on its own (without any assistance from the child).

Straw Tower
● **Glad Drinking Straws** and **Scotch Tape.** Build towers and bridges with a box of Glad Drinking Straws and a roll of Scotch Tape. For a party game, divide children into teams, give each team a box of straws and a roll of tape, and instruct them to build the tallest freestanding tower possible within twenty minutes—without talking. You'll learn that success requires proper communication, and you'll have to figure out how to work together.

Toothpick Bridge
● **Forster Toothpicks** and **Elmer's Glue-All.** With box of Forster Toothpicks and a bottle of Elmer's Glue-All, you can construct buildings, walls, bridges, and towers. For a real challenge, use two boxes of toothpicks to build a bridge capable of spanning an eighteen-inch gap and supporting a weight of ten pounds placed the middle of the bridge—for at least ten seconds.

STRANGE FACTS

● In 1173, an unknown architect designed a ten-foot thick foundation for the bell tower in the Italian town of Pisa, but when construction on the tower began in 1174, the ground shifted and the building started leaning. Construction was halted for a hundred years, and the tower was completed in 1350 with the top tier built out of line with the rest of the tower in a vain attempt to correct the tilt. Tilting an average of one-quarter inch per year, the tower has shifted seventeen feet from the perpendicular. In 1934, the Italian government pumped concrete under the base to stop further tilting, but that project actually sped up the tilting. In 1982, the Italian government spent $10.5 million in an attempt to stop the tilting. Eventually the tower will topple over, though predictions vary widely as to precisely when.

● Two towers built in 1488 in Bologna, standing less than twenty feet apart, lean in opposite directions. The Torre degli Asinelli, a 320-foot tall tower in the center of the Piazza di Porta Ravegnana leans 7.5 feet from the perpendicular. Its twin tower, the Torre Garisenda, tilts ten feet.

● British civil engineer Sir Thomas Bouch designed a two-mile-long bridge to cross the Tay River in Scotland from Newport to Dundee. The bridge was opened in 1878, and Bouch was knighted in June 1879. Unfortunately, Bouch did not make any provisions for the bridge to withstand the effects of wind pressure, nor did he provide any continuous lateral wind bracing below the deck. On December 28, 1879, a hurricane hit the bridge, blowing thirteen spans of wrought-iron lattice girders into the river, bringing the Edinburgh mail train with them, killing all seventy passengers aboard.

● On November 7, 1940, four months after the ribbon was cut on the $6.5 million Tacoma Narrows Bridge in Washington, a 42-mile-per-hour wind created oscillations in the suspension bridge (then the third longest in the world), tearing several suspenders loose and causing the single 2800-foot span to break apart and fall into Puget Sound. Engineers had designed "Galloping Gertie" without taking into account aerodynamic effects and other structural weaknesses.

Toys

Ball and Bucket Game
● **Clorox Bleach jugs.** With adult supervision, cut the bottoms and one side diagonally up to the handle on two clean, empty Clorox Bleach jugs. Put a ball in one catcher and toss to your partner who catches it in the other bleach bottle. You can also decorate the catchers.

Beanbags
● **L'eggs Sheer Energy Panty Hose** and **Uncle Ben's Converted Brand Rice.** Cut off the feet from a pair of clean, used L'eggs Sheer Energy Panty Hose, fill each foot with Uncle Ben's Converted Brand Rice, and tie a knot in the open end. You can use these beanbags to play catch. Or with adult supervision, cut a hole in a medium-sized corrugated cardboard box, paint that side of the box with a clown or animal face, and play bean-bag toss (see page 64).

Bicycle Power
● **Forster Clothes Pins.** To give a bicycle the roar of a motorcycle, use Forster Clothes Pins to clip playing cards to the beams that hold the bicycle wheels in place so that the cards are held into the spokes.

Boat
● **Ivory Soap** and **Forster Toothpicks.** Carve a boat from a bar of Ivory Soap. Use a Forster toothpick to add a sail cut from a piece of colored construction paper. Ivory Soap floats in the bathtub. For more tips on how to carve soap, see page 119.

Building Bricks
● **Con-Tact Paper.** Cover empty shoeboxes with Con-Tact Paper to create building bricks.

Mail Box

● **Quaker Oats.** Decorate a clean, empty Quaker Oats canister with colored construction paper, glue, crayons, and glitter to make a toy mail box.

Marble Maze

● **Glad Drinking Straws** and **Elmer's Glue-All.** With adult supervision, use a pair of scissors to cut several Glad Drinking Straws into pieces of various lengths. Use Elmer's Glue-All to glue the straws to the bottom of the inside of a shallow cardboard box to create a maze with paths wide enough for a marble to pass through. You can cut a hole in the side of the box to insert the marble and a second hole at the end of the maze for the marble to exit the box. When the glue dries, place a marble in the box and tilt the box to run the marble through the maze.

Miniature Kite

● **Oral-B Dental Floss, Glad Drinking Straws, Ziploc Storage Bags, Scotch Tape,** and **Glad Trash Bags.** Thread a long piece of Oral-B Dental Floss through three Glad Drinking Straws and tie a secure knot to form a triangle. Using another piece of dental floss, add two more straws to form a second triangle alongside the first, knotting securely. Using one last piece of dental floss, add one more straw to form a third triangle, creating a tetrahedron, again knotting securely. Cut open the side seams of the Ziploc Storage bag so you have one flat piece of clear plastic. Place the straw tetrahedron on top of the plastic as a guide with adult supervision

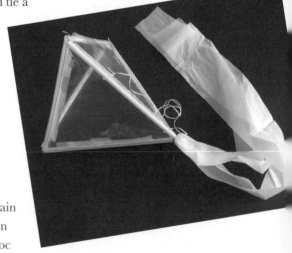

use a pair of scissors to carefully cut the plastic so it will cover two triangular sides of the tetrahedron, allowing for an additional inch of plastic along each edge of the plastic. Using Scotch Tape, tape the plastic over two sides of the kite frame. To attach the string to the kite, cut a 24-inch length of dental floss. Tie one end of the floss through the plastic and around the straw in the center of the plastic sheet, about three inches from the end of the straw. Tie the free end of the floss through the plastic and around the straw one-half inch from the other end of the straw. To prevent the floss from slipping and tearing the plastic, use a piece of Scotch Tape to secure the floss to the straw in both spots inside the kite. Tie the end of a roll of kite string (or a roll of dental floss) to the center of the bridle (the loop of dental floss you just attached to the kite) and knot securely. Create a tail for the kite by cutting a strip of plastic two inches wide by three feet long from a Glad Trash Bag. Using a short piece of dental floss, attach the tail to the bottom of the kite near the second bridle string. The temperature, wind speed, and humidity affect how well the kite flies, so be prepared to adjust the length of the tail or the bridle string to get the kite to fly to your liking.

Parachute Toy

● **Glad Trash Bags, Hula Hoop,** and **Oral-B Dental Floss.** To make a toy parachute, with adult supervision, use a pair of scissors to cut open a Glad Trash Bag along one of the side seams and along the bottom seam. Place the open trash bag on a flat surface and lay a Hula Hoop on top of the sheet of plastic. With an indelible marker, trace around the Hula Hoop to make a circle. Use the scissors to cut out the circle of plastic. Using a hole puncher, punch a hole in the plastic one inch in from the edge of the circle. Thinking of the first hole as twelve o'clock on a clock face, punch a second hole at three o'clock, a third hole at six o'clock, and a fourth hole at nine o'clock. Cut four two-foot lengths of Oral-B Dental Floss (or string). Tie one end of a two-foot length of string through each hole. Tie the free ends of the four strings together through a metal washer (one-inch in diameter). Fold up the plastic parachute, wrap the string around it, and toss it up into the air.

Pinwheel

● **Reynolds Wrap, Glad Drinking Straws,** and **Scotch Tape.**
To make a pinwheel, cut a six-inch square of Reynolds Wrap, fold it in
half diagonally, and then fold it in half diagonally again. Open up the
folded square, poke a pinhole in the center, and cut along the diagonal
folds toward the center, leaving an uncut X with one-inch legs in
the center. Bend two opposite petals forward and the remaining two
opposite petals backward so that all four corners overlap the center
hole. With adult supervision, push a straight pin through the four
corners and the center hole. Poke the pin through the end of a Glad
Drinking Straw, bend the sharp end down, and secure to the straw
with Scotch Tape.

Playhouse

● **Con-Tact Paper.** To create your own playhouse or fort, with adult
supervision, cut doors and windows out of a large cardboard box and
then decorate the house or fort with Con-Tact Paper.

Sand Scooper and Pail

● **Clorox Bleach jug.** With adult supervision, cut an empty, clean
Clorox Bleach jug in half. Use the half with the handle as a scooper
and use the bottom half as a small bucket.

Snow Globe

● **Gerber Baby Food jar, Krazy Glue,** and **Scotch Packaging
Tape.** Make a "snow"-filled paperweight by using Krazy Glue to
attach a small plastic figurine to the inside bottom of a clean, empty
Gerber Baby Food jar. When the glue dries, fill the jar three-quarters
full with water, add a teaspoon of silver glitter, screw on the cap, and
seal with clear Scotch Packaging Tape.

Stilts

● **Maxwell House Coffee cans.** With adult supervision, punch
two holes each in the closed end of two empty Maxwell House Coffee
cans. String rope through the holes to create a loop for each can,
creating a pair of stilts.

Stress Ball

● **Gold Medal Flour.** Stretch a balloon a few times, insert a funnel in the neck of the balloon, fill the balloon with Gold Medal Flour, and tie a knot. If flour gets stuck in the funnel, use a pencil to gently poke the flour through the hole. You can use the ball for juggling, playing catch, or as a hackeysack.. Or loan it to your parents for use as a stress ball. To relieve stress, simply squeeze the flour-filled balloon.

Time Capsule

● **Quaker Oats.** Decorate a clean, empty Quaker Oats canister and use it as a time capsule. Fill it with photos, art projects, and letters and toys, books, and jewelry that you've outgrown. Date and label the time capsule and stash it in a closet to reopen at a later date.

Toy Logs

● **Quaker Oats** and **Con-Tact Paper.** Create toy logs by covering clean, empty Quaker Oats canisters with Con-Tact Paper with a wood-grain design.

Weight Lifting

● **Clorox Bleach jug.** Make dumbbells by filling two empty, clean Clorox Bleach jugs with sand or water and sealing the caps securely. To make the dumbbells lighter, just pour out some of the water.

STRANGE FACTS

● In the 1870s, William Russell Frisbie opened a bakery called the Frisbie Pie Company in Bridgeport, Connecticut. His lightweight pie tins were embossed with the family name. In the mid-1940s, students at Yale University tossed the empty pie tins as a game. In the 1950s, Walter Frederick Morrison, a Los Angeles building inspector determined to capitalize on Hollywood's obsession with UFOs, designed a lightweight plastic disk, based on the Frisbie bakery's pie tins, but changed the name to Flyin' Saucer to avoid legal hassles. Morrison sold the rights to the Wham-O Manufacturing Co. of San Gabriel, California, and on January 13, 1957, Wham-O launched the

Frisbee. In 1958, the Frisbie Pie Company went out of business, but its
pie tins live on, reincarnated as the Frisbee.

● Middlebury College in Vermont insists that the Frisbee got its start
on the Middlebury campus. In 1989, the college unveiled a bronze
statue of a dog jumping to catch a Frisbee to commemorate the
alleged fiftieth anniversary of the Frisbee.

● In 1916, John Lloyd Wright, inspired by the interlocking building
system used to construct Tokyo's earthquake-proof Imperial Hotel
(designed by his father, architect Frank Lloyd Wright), developed a
toy building set comprised of sturdy, interlocking logs made from real
wood. Wright named the construction set Lincoln Logs after President
Abraham Lincoln (who was born in a log cabin), in honor of the
fiftieth anniversary of the end of the Civil War.

● In 1943, Richard James, a 29-year-old marine engineer working in
Philadelphia's Cramp Shipyard, tried to figure out how to use springs
to mount delicate meters for testing horsepower on World War II
battleships. When a torsion spring fell off his desk and tumbled end
over end across the floor, James realized he could create a new toy by
devising a steel formula that would give the spring the proper tension
to "walk." After James found a steel wire that would coil, uncoil,
and recoil, his wife Betty thumbed through the dictionary to find
an appropriate name for the toy. She chose Slinky because it meant
"stealthy, sleek, and sinuous."

Acknowledgments

At Fair Winds Press, I am grateful to my editor Ellen Phillips for her passion, enthusiasm, and excitement for this book. I am also deeply indebted to my publisher Holly Schmidt, researcher and photo shoot producer Debbie Green, expert copy editor Jennifer Bright Reich, art director Rosalind Wanke, cover photographer Ken Chernus, senior designer Claire MacMaster, marketing and publicity director Mary Aarons, publicist Liz Polay-Wettengel, managing editor John Gettings, editorial assistant Alexis Sullivan, proofreader Jacqueline Brownstein, and talented supermodels Julia Green and Ari Vogel.

A very special thanks to my agent Jeremy Solomon, my manager Barb North, and to the hundreds of people who continually visit my Web site and send me their ingenious ideas.

Above all, all my love to Debbie, Ashley, and Julia.

The Fine Print

Sources

● *Another Use For* by Vicki Lansky (Deephaven, Minnesota: Book Peddlers, 1991)

● *The Art of Batik* by members of the Batik Guild (Wales: The Batik Guild, 1999)

● *The Big Book of Fun and Great Things to Do and Learn* edited by Lucy Painter (London: Anness Publishing, 1999)

● *The Book of Lists* by David Wallechinsky, Irving Wallace, and Amy Wallace (New York: Bantam, 1977)

● *Can It Really Rain Frogs?* by Spencer Christian (New York: John Wiley & Sons, 1997)

● *The Colossal Book of Crafts for Kids and Their Families* by Phyllis Fiarotta with Noel Fiarotta (New York: Black Dog & Leventhal Publishers, 1997)

● *Crafts to Make in the Summer* by Kathy Ross and illustrated by Vicky Enright (Brookfield, Connecticut: Millbrook Press, 1999)

● *Dictionary of Trade Name Origins* by Adrian Room (London: Routledge & Kegan Paul, 1982)

● *The Dorling Kindersley Science Encyclopedia* (New York: Dorling Kindersley, 1994)

● *Einstein's Science Parties* by Shar Levine and Allison Grafton (New York: John Wiley & Sons, 1994)

● *Eyewitness Books: Crystal and Gem* by R. F. Symes and R. R. Harding (New York: Knopf, 1991)

● *Famous American Trademarks* by Arnold B. Barach (Washington, D.C.: Public Affairs Press, 1971)

● *The Guinness Book of Records* edited by Peter Matthews (New York: Bantam, 1993)

● *How in the World?* by the editors of *Reader's Digest* (Pleasantville, New York: Reader's Digest, 1990)

- *I Can Make That!: Fantastic Crafts for Kids* by Mary Wallace (Toronto: Maple Tree Press, 2002)
- *Janice VanCleave's 200 Gooey, Slippery, Slimy, Weird & Fun Experiments* by Janice VanCleave (New York: John Wiley & Sons, 1993)
- *Jewelry Making* by Jo Moody (Laguna Hills, California: Walter Foster, 1998)
- *Jr. Boom Academy* by B. K. Hixson and M. S. Kralik (Salt Lake City, Utah: Wild Goose, 1992)
- *Kids' Crazy Concoctions: 50 Mysterious Mixtures for Art & Craft Fun* by Jill Frankel Hauser and illustrated by Loretta Trezzo Braren (Charlotte, Vermont: Williamson, 1995)
- *Look What You Can Make with Dozens of Household Items!* edited by Kathy Ross (Honesdale, Pennsylvania: Boyds Mills Press, 2001)
- *Marbling* by Diane Vogel Maurer with Paul Maurer (New York: Friedman Fairfax, 1994)
- *Marbling Techniques* by Wendy Addison Medeiros (New York: Watson-Guptill, 1994)
- *Martin Gardner's Science Tricks* by Martin Gardner (New York: Sterling, 1998)
- *Mary Ellen's Best of Helpful Hints* by Mary Ellen Pinkham (New York: Warner/B. Lansky, 1979)
- *Mary Ellen's Greatest Hints* by Mary Ellen Pinkham (New York: Fawcett Crest, 1990)
- "More Than You Want to Know About SPAM" by Judith Stone (*New York Times Magazine*, July 3, 1994)
- *100 Amazing Make-It-Yourself Science Fair Projects* by Glen Vecchione (New York: Sterling, 1995)
- *The Outrageously Big Activity, Play and Project Book* edited by Joanne Hanks (New York: Anness Publishing, 1998)
- *Paint!* by Kim Solga (Cincinatti, Ohio: F&W Publications, 1991)
- *Paints Plus* by Gillian Souter (Milwaukee, Wisconsin: Gareth Stevens, 2001)
- *Panati's Extraordinary Origins of Everyday Things* by Charles Panati (New York: HarperCollins, 1987)
- *Paper Art* by Diane Maurer-Mathison with Jennifer Philippoff (New York: Watson-Guptill, 1997)

● *Paper Craft School* by Clive Stevens (Pleasantville, New York: Reader's Digest, 1996)

● *Practical Problem Solver* by the editors of *Reader's Digest* (Pleasantville, New York: Reader's Digest, 1991)

● *Reader's Digest Book of Facts* edited by Edmund H. Harvey, Jr. (Pleasantville, New York: Reader's Digest, 1987)

● *Recipes for Art and Craft Materials* by Helen Roney Sattler (New York: Beech Tree Books, 1994)

● *Science Fair Survival Techniques* (Salt Lake City, Utah: Wild Goose, 1997)

● *Science for Fun Experiments* by Gary Gibson (Brookfield, Connecticut: Copper Beech Books, 1996)

● *Science Wizardry for Kids* by Margaret Kenda and Phyllis S. Williams (Hauppauge, New York: Barron's, 1992)

● *Shake, Rattle and Roll* by Spencer Christian (New York: John Wiley & Sons, 1997)

● *Steven Caney's Toy Book* by Steven Caney (New York: Workman, 1972)

● *The Tabasco Cookbook* by Paul McIlhenny with Barbara Hunter (New York: Clarkson Potter, 1993)

● *333 Science Tricks & Experiments* by Robert J. Brown (Blue Ridge Summit, Pennsylvania: TAB Books, 1984)

● *365 Simple Science Experiments* by E. Richard Churchill, Louis V. Loeschnig, and Muriel Mandell (New York: Black Dog & Leventhal, 1997)

● *365 Things to Make and Do* by Vivienne Bolton (Bristol, England: Dempsey Parr, 1998)

● *200 Illustrated Science Experiments for Children* by Robert J. Brown (Blue Ridge Summit, Pennsylvania: TAB Books, 1987)

● *The Usborne Book of Art Ideas* by Fiona Watt (Tulsa, Oklahoma: Educational Development Corporation, 1999)

● *What Makes the Grand Canyon Grand?* by Spencer Christian (New York: John Wiley & Sons, 1998)

● *Why Did They Name It . . . ?* by Hannah Campbell (New York: Fleet, 1964)

Trademark Information

"Albers" is a registered trademark of Nestlé Food Company.

"Alberto VO5" is a registered trademark of Alberto-Culver USA, Inc.

"Alka-Seltzer" is a registered trademark of Miles, Inc.

"Aqua Net is a registered trademark of Faberge USA Inc.

"Arm & Hammer" is a registered trademark of Church & Dwight Co, Inc.

"Betty Crocker" and "Potato Buds" are registered trademarks of General Mills, Inc.

"Birds Eye" is a registered trademark of Birds Eye Foods.

"Blue Bonnet" is a registered trademark of Unilever.

"Bounce" is a registered trademark of Procter & Gamble.

"Bounty" is a registered trademark of Procter & Gamble.

"Bubble Wrap" is a registered trademark of Sealed Air Corporation.

"Budweiser" is a registered trademark of Anheuser-Busch, Inc.

"C&H" is a registered trademark of C&H Sugar Company, Inc.

"Campbell" is a registered trademark of Campbell Soup Company.

"Canada Dry" is a registered trademark of Cadbury Beverages Inc.

"Carnation" is a registered trademark of Nestlé Food Company.

"Cascade" is a registered trademark of Procter & Gamble.

"Charmin" is a registered trademark of Procter & Gamble.

"Cheerios" is a registered trademark of General Mills, Inc.

"Clairol" and "Herbal Essences" are registered trademarks of Clairol.

"Clorox" is a registered trademark of The Clorox Company.

"Close-Up" is a registered trademark of Chesebrough-Ponds USA, Co.

"Coca-Cola" and "Coke" are registered trademarks of the Coca-Cola Company.

"Colgate" is a registered trademark of Colgate-Palmolive.

"Con-Tact" is a registered trademark of Newell Rubbermaid.

"Conair" and "Pro Style" are registered trademarks of Conair Corporation.

"Cool Whip" is a registered trademark of Kraft Foods.

"Country Time" and "Country Time Lemonade" are registered trademarks of Dr Pepper/Seven Up, Inc.

"Cover Girl" and "NailSlicks" are registered trademarks of Procter & Gamble.

"Crayola" is a registered trademark of Binney & Smith Inc.

"Crisco" is a registered trademark of Procter & Gamble.

"Cutex" is a registered trademark of MedTech Products Inc.

"Dannon" is a registered trademark of the Dannon Company.

"Dawn" is a registered trademark of Procter & Gamble.

"Dixie" is a registered trademark of Georgia-Pacific.

"Downy" is a registered trademark of Procter & Gamble.

"Elmer's Glue-All" and Elmer the Bull are registered trademarks of Borden.

"Energizer" is a registered trademark of Energizer Holdings, Inc.

"Era" is a registered trademark of Procter & Gamble.

"Fleischman's" is a registered trademark of ACH Food Companies, Inc.

"Forster" is a registered trademark of Diamond Brands, Inc.

"French's" is a registered trademark of Reckitt Benckiser.

"Frisbee" is a registered trademark of WHAM-O Inc.

"Gatorade" is a registered trademark of The Gatorade Company.

"Gerber" is a registered trademark of Gerber Products Co.

"Gillette" and "Foamy" are registered trademarks of Gillette.

"Glad" is a registered trademark of First Brands Corporation.

"Gold Medal" is a registered trademark of General Mills, Inc.

"Hartz" is a registered trademark of The Hartz Mountain Corporation.

"Heinz" is a registered trademark of H.J. Heinz Company.

"Hershey's" is a registered trademark of Hershey Foods Corporation.

"Honey Maid" is a registered trademark of Nabisco.

"Huggies" is a registered trademark of Kimberly-Clark Corporation.

"Hula Hoop" is a registered trademark of WHAM-O Inc.

"Ivory" is a registered trademark of Procter & Gamble.

"Jell-O" is a registered trademark of Kraft Foods, Inc.

"Jet-Puffed" is a registered trademark of Kraft Foods, Inc.

"Jif" is a registered trademark of Procter & Gamble.

"Johnson's" and "Johnson & Johnson" are registered trademarks of Johnson & Johnson.

"Joy" is a registered trademark of Procter & Gamble.

"Karo" is a registered trademark of CPC International Inc.

"Kellogg's" and "Froot Loops" are registered trademarks of the Kellogg Company.

"Kingsford's" and the Kingsford logo are registered trademarks of ACH Food Companies.

"Kiwi" is a registered trademark of Sara Lee Corporation.

"Kleenex" is a registered trademark of Kimberly-Clark Corporation.

"Knox" is a registered trademark of NBTY, Inc.

"Kodak" is a registered trademark of Eastman Kodak Company.

"Kool-Aid" is a registered trademark of Kraft Foods.

"Kraft" and "Handi-Snacks" are registered trademarks of Kraft Foods.

"Krazy" is a registered trademark of Borden, Inc.

"L'eggs" and "Sheer Energy" are registered trademarks of Sara Lee

Corporation.

"Land O Lakes" is a registered trademark of Land O Lakes, Inc.

"Lipton" is a registered trademark of the Thomas J. Lipton Company.

"Listerine" is a registered trademark of Warner-Lambert.

"Lubriderm" is a registered trademark of Warner-Lambert.

"M&M's" is a registered trademark of Mars, Incorporated.

"Maxwell House" is a registered trademark of Maxwell House Coffee Company.

"McCormick" is a registered trademark of McCormick & Company, Incorporated.

"Miracle Whip" is a registered trademark of Kraft Foods, Inc.

"Morton" and the Morton Umbrella Girl are registered trademarks of Morton International, Inc.

"Mr. Coffee" is a registered trademark of Mr. Coffee, Inc.

"Mrs. Stewart's" is a registered trademark of Luther Ford & Co.

"Murine Tears" is a registered trademark of Prestige Brands, Inc.

"Murphy" is a registered trademark of Colgate-Palmolive Company.

"Noxzema" is a registered trademark of Procter & Gamble.

"Oral-B" is a registered trademark of Oral-B Laboratories.

"Orville Redenbacher's Gourmet" and "Popping Corn" are registered trademarks of ConAgra Foods.

"Pam" is a registered trademark of American Home Foods.

"Pampers" is a registered trademark of Procter & Gamble.

"Parsons'" is a registered trademark of Church & Dwight Co., Inc.

"Pepperidge Farm" is a registered trademark of PF Brands, Inc.

"Phillips'" is a registered trademark of Bayer Corporation.

"Playtex" and "Living" are registered trademarks of Playtex Products, Inc.

"Pond's" is a registered trademark of Unilever.

"Post Alpha-Bits" is a registered trademark of Kraft Foods.

"Pringles" is a registered trademark of Procter & Gamble.

"Purell" is a registered trademark of Gojo Industries, Inc.

"Q-Tips" is a registered trademark of Chesebrough-Pond's USA Co.

"Quaker Oats" is a registered trademark of the Quaker Oats Company.

"ReaLemon" is a registered trademark of Mott's Inc.

"Reddi-wip" is a registered trademark of Con Agra Foods, Inc.

"Reynolds Wrap" and "Cut-Rite" are registered trademarks of Reynolds Metals.

"Rubbermaid" is a registered trademark of Rubbermaid.

"Saran Wrap" is a registered trademark of S.C. Johnson & Son, Inc.

"Scotch" and "3M" are registered trademarks of 3M.

"7-Up" is a registered trademark of Dr Pepper/Seven-Up, Inc.

"Silly Putty" is a registered trademark of Binney & Smith Inc.

"Slinky" is a registered trademark of James Industries.

"SPAM" is a registered trademark of Hormel Foods Corporation.

"Sta-Flo" is a registered trademark of the Dial Corporation.

"SueBee" is a registered trademark of Sioux Honey Association.

"Sun-Maid" is a registered trademark of Sun-Maid Growers of California.

"Tabasco" is a registered trademark of McIlhenny Company.

"Tang" is a registered trademark of Kraft Foods.

"Tide" is a registered trademark of Procter & Gamble.

"Tupperware" is a registered trademark of Tupperware Worldwide.

"20 Mule Team" and "Borax" are registered trademarks of United States Borax & Chemical Corporation.

"Uncle Ben's" and "Converted" are registered trademarks of Uncle Ben's, Inc.

"*USA Today*" is a registered trademark of Gannett News Service.

"Vaseline" is a registered trademark of the Chesebrough-Pond's USA Co.

"Velcro" is a registered trademark of Velcro Industries.

"WD-40" is a registered trademark of the WD-40 Company.

"Welch's" is a trademark of Welch Foods Inc.

"Wesson" is a registered trademark of Hunt-Wesson, Inc.

"Wilson" is a registered trademark of Wilson Sporting Goods Co.

"Windex" is a registered trademark of S. C. Johnson & Sons, Inc.

"Wonder" is a registered trademark of Interstate Brands Corporation.

"Ziploc" is a registered trademark of S. C. Johnson & Sons, Inc.

Index

About the Author

Joey Green—author of *Polish Your Furniture with Panty Hose, Paint Your House with Powdered Milk, Wash Your Hair with Whipped Cream,* and *Clean Your Clothes with Cheez Whiz*—got Jay Leno to shave with Jif Peanut Butter on *The Tonight Show,* Rosie O'Donnell to mousse her hair with Jell-O on *The Rosie O'Donnell Show,* and had Katie Couric drop her  diamond engagement ring in a glass of Efferdent on *Today.* He has been seen polishing furniture with SPAM on *NBC Dateline,* cleaning a toilet with Coca-Cola in the *New York Times,* and washing his hair with Reddi-wip in *People.* Green, a former contributing editor to *National Lampoon* and a former advertising copywriter at J. Walter Thompson, is the author of thirty-five books, including *Marx & Lennon: The Parallel Sayings, Weird Christmas,* and *The Zen of Oz: Ten Spiritual Lessons from Over the Rainbow.* A native of Miami, Florida, and a graduate of Cornell University, he wrote television commercials for Burger King and Walt Disney World and won a Clio Award for a print ad he created for Eastman Kodak. He backpacked around the world for two years on his honeymoon and lives in Los Angeles with his wife, Debbie, and their two daughters, Ashley and Julia.

**Visit Joey Green on the Internet at
www.wackyuses.com**